Vicente Huidobro
Uncollected

Also available in this series

Poetry

Selected Poems

Adam / Adán
Square Horizon / Horizon carré
Equatorial & other poems
Arctic Poems / Poemas árticos
Painted Poems *
Paris 1925: Ordinary Autumn & All of a Sudden / Automne régulier & Tout à coup
Altazor *
Skyquake / Temblor de cielo
Citizen of Oblivion / El ciudadano del olvido
Seeing and Touching / Ver y palpar
Last Poems / Últimos poemas

Fiction

El Cid / Mío Cid Campeador
Cagliostro
Three Huge Novels / Tres novelas inmensas
Papa, or The Diary of Alicia Mir / Papa, o el diario de Alicia Mir *
Satyr, or The Power of Words / Sátiro, o el poder le la palabra

Other Prose

Manifestos
Adverse Winds / Vientos contrarios

Volodia Teitelboim: *Vicente Huidobro — in perpetual motion: A Biography*

* *a volume yet to appear at the time this book was published*

Vicente Huidobro

Uncollected Poems

Poemas inéditos

Translated from Spanish & French by
Tony Frazer

Shearsman Books

First published in the United Kingdom in 2025 by
Shearsman Books Ltd
PO Box 4239
Swindon
SN3 9FN

Shearsman Books Ltd Registered Office
30–31 St. James Place, Mangotsfield, Bristol BS16 9JB
(this address not for correspondence)

www.shearsman.com

EU AUTHORISED REPRESENTATIVE:
Lightning Source France,
1 Av. Johannes Gutenberg, 78310 Maurepas, France
Email: compliance@lightningsource.fr

ISBN 978-1-84861-818-3

CONTENTS

Occasional Poems

Uncollected French Poems

ACKNOWLEDGEMENTS

The original texts of most of the poems in this volume are based on several sources but, most importantly, on those printed in the author's *Obra poética* [Poetic Works], edited by Cedomil Goic (Paris: Éditions ALLCA XX, 2003). Further details are available in the Appendix to this volume.

The translation of 'Passion Passion and Death' first appeared in an earlier version in Vicente Huidobro, *Selected Poems* (first edition), edited by Tony Frazer, and translated by various hands (Bristol: Shearsman Books, 2019).

'Canto to Lindbergh'

Huidobro, V. (1927). Manuscrito de 'Canto to Lindbergh' [manuscrito mecanografiado]. Archivo Fundación Vicente Huidobro UC, Biblioteca de Humanidades de la Pontificia Universidad Católica de Chile.

We are most grateful to the Huidobro Foundation and to the Universidad Católica de Chile for their assistance in this matter, for their provision of the scanned typescripts, and for their kind permission to reproduce them in this volume. The existence of two different versions of the translation was a welcome surprise.

For permission to reproduce the scanned newspaper images of 'Canto a Lindbergh' we are grateful to Pedro Marqués de Armas, his blog *Hotel Telégrafo*, and the associated press Potemkin Ediciones, which first published them in a PDF eBook, *Vicente Huidobro: Pasajes para cien poetas*, in July 2024.

Finally, we are grateful to the Getty Research Institute, Los Angeles, for providing the scan of 'Demande votre mort', and their permission to reproduce it within these pages.

INTRODUCTION

Vicente Huidobro was born in Santiago de Chile in 1893; he died of a brain hæmorrhage in Cartagena, Chile on 2 January 1948, a few days before his fifty-fifth birthday.

Huidobro came from a wealthy patrician family. Unlike many youths of his age and class, Huidobro dedicated himself to literature. 'At the age of seventeen,' he was to write in 1926, 'I said to myself: "I must be the first poet of America"; then, as the years passed, I said: "I must be the first poet of my language"; finally, my ambitions soared and I said to myself: "I have to be the first poet of my century".' Modesty was not one of Huidobro's defining characteristics.

After some early literary successes and the publication of several books, Huidobro left Chile with his family in late 1916, bound first for Madrid, and then for Paris. While he very much wanted to see what was happening in the world's artistic capital, the initial impetus for the move had in fact been the avoidance of further scandal at home, from which Huidobro had not long before disappeared to Buenos Aires with Teresa Wilms Montt (1893–1921). The pair certainly seem to have had an affair, but the event also had a rather more gentlemanly aspect, as Huidobro had engineered Teresa's escape from the Santiago convent in which she had been immured by her irate husband, following her affair with one of his cousins. Teresa was to develop her own literary career in Buenos Aires and would later move on to Europe, where she was to commit suicide in 1921. Huidobro continued to remember her long afterwards, and the daring escape to Argentina prefigured his later exploits with Ximena Amunátegui, who was to become his second, albeit common-law, wife.

In Paris he threw himself into the artistic avant-garde, getting involved with a Cubist magazine, *Nord-Sud*, edited by Pierre Reverdy, and establishing friendships with Juan Gris, Picasso, Picabia and Lipchitz, as well as with poets such as Apollinaire, Cendrars and Cocteau. In July of 1918, to escape the war, he moved to Madrid where he participated in the *tertulia* (literary salon) of Ramón Gómez de la Serna at the Café Pombo; he also came into contact with significant young writers there such as Gerardo Diego, Jorge Luis Borges and Juan Larrea.

In 1918 Huidobro was obliged to return to Chile for his sister's wedding. He hoped to take literary Santiago by storm but instead met with a blank wall of conservatism and indifference. He went back to Paris in 1920 and, in 1921, published a selected poems, *Saisons choisies* [Selected Seasons], accompanied by a statement of his own aesthetic principles, 'La Création pure'. But Huidobro's Creationism—a kind of literary cubism, which argued for the independence of artistic works from observable reality—was soon overtaken by Surrealism and the craze for automatic writing, which he rejected as 'the reduction of poetry to a simple, after-dinner, family pastime'. Creationism was a useful label, a marketing slogan in modern terms, under which attention was sought, and gained. As is still the case today, commentators happily discussed the supposedly attendant artistic theories rather than the works that exemplified them.

In 1925, political changes in Chile attracted his attention and Huidobro, always thinking in the grandest terms, saw an opportunity to become the political leader of a new Chile. Even his mother fantasised about her son as King Vicente I of Chile. The (pipe)dream of a Huidobro monarchy, however, was not to be realised, and his run for the presidency of the republic faltered well before the elections. In 1925 he had also issued two further collections of poetry in French, *Automne régulier* [Ordinary Autumn] and *Tout à coup* [All of a Sudden], two experimental dead-ends, which show him trying out Dada and Surrealism, notwithstanding his imprecations against the latter, although more positive signs of development were in fact to be found as, at the same period, he started publishing sections from the work-in-progress *Altazor*, in Spanish, in literary journals.

Huidobro had married young, to Manuela Portales Bello (1894–1965), likewise the scion of a famous patrician family, with whom he had four children and from whom he later separated to form a new and scandalous relationship with the sixteen-year-old Ximena Amunátegui (1912–1975), a relative by marriage (sister of a sister-in-law) with whom he would go on to have a fifth child. The beginnings of this relationship, in which, after meeting her at a costume ball, Huidobro published a long love poem, 'Pasión y muerte' [Passion and Death] in Santiago's *La Nación* newspaper on Good Friday, obliged Huidobro to leave Chile, first for Paris, then for New York in 1927 where he came close to becoming involved in the film business. He met Douglas Fairbanks and Gloria Swanson, and even won a prize of US$10,000 (some $150,000 in today's dollars) for his film-script, *Cagliostro* – later converted into a novella – as being the best candidate for a new movie. Nothing came of this, because of the arrival of the *talkies* shortly afterwards, which immediately rendered the expressionist silent style of *Cagliostro* out of date.

Huidobro's former associates in the Parisian avant-garde evidently saw the furore over a teenage paramour, and the abortive presidential campaign, as signs of madness or, at the very least, an early-onset mid-life crisis. It is not clear what they would have thought of the press photos of Huidobro with Hollywood starlets, although one can hazard a guess.

When Ximena reached her majority in 1928, Huidobro left New York and travelled secretly to Chile where he scooped her up from outside her convent school – as a subterfuge, she had sought permission from the nuns to go to the dentist – and the pair fled to Argentina. A former family maid had acted as go-between for the pair. Within a few months the couple resurfaced in Paris where they were allegedly married in a Muslim ceremony, a Christian ceremony being out of the question given that Vicente remained legally married to Manuela. During the following years in Paris Huidobro completed his two major works, *Altazor* and *Temblor de cielo* [Skyquake] – although, according to the author, the former was begun some years before – as well as the novel *Mío Cid Campeador* (available in this series under the title *El Cid*).

In 1932 the changed economic realities subsequent to the great Crash necessitated Huidobro's return to Chile. Politically at this time, he was a man of the Left, although in the 1940s he would become anti-Communist. At the outbreak of the Spanish Civil War, Huidobro organised Chilean intellectuals in support of the Republic and in 1937 he was in Spain, with Líster's troops on the Aragón front and took part in pro-Republican literary conferences in Madrid and Valencia.

By the end of the 1930s, however, Huidobro was thoroughly disillusioned with politics, which he described as 'the art of lying, of concealing, of falsifying, of dirtying life, of buying and selling consciences'. He was also deeply affected by the death of his mother, and a few years later by the collapse of his second marriage: Ximena had found new love with a younger suitor, the Argentine-born poet and architect Godofredo Iommi (1917–2001), going on to marry him after her separation from Huidobro – a divorce not being required, as her union with Vicente never had any legal standing.

Escaping these events, Huidobro went to France in 1944 as a war correspondent for newspapers in Montevideo and Buenos Aires and was with the Allied troops in Germany, even broadcasting from Paris on The Voice of America. During the war Huidobro was wounded twice and was obliged to go to London for medical treatment. When at last, in 1945, he returned to Chile it was with a new partner, Raquel Señoret (1922–1990), who had previously been married to the English writer, John Watney, and was the daughter of the late Chilean Ambassador to the United Kingdom. The couple set up home in Cartagena, a coastal resort south of Valparaíso, where Vicente had inherited a property. In the short time left to him, he took little interest in contemporary Chilean poetry.

* * *

The above summary of Vicente Huidobro's life does little justice to one of the most flamboyant, gifted and relentlessly innovative poets of the 20th century. His literary theories are best presented as expounded by himself in his manifestos (also available in this series). He had the grandest notion of the function of the poet, and he did his best to live up to it. His literary presence is still felt in Latin American poetry and, as with his contemporary, the great Peruvian poet, César Vallejo, there is a growing appreciation of his work in the English-speaking world. His poetry is wonderfully experimental, sometimes outrageous, narcissistic, and egotistical in a quasi-Whitmanesque fashion, but it constitutes a splendid corrective to our sometimes lazy view of the trajectory of 20th-century poetry. It is my firm conviction that, warts and all, Huidobro is one of the defining figures of 20th century Hispanic poetry.

* * *

The current volume includes all the poems by Huidobro – that I have been able to trace – which did not appear in any of his formal, mature collections, and which have not already been included as appendices, or variant texts, in other books in this series. I date the author's "maturity" from the volume *Adam* (Santiago, 1916, but written in 1914), though I readily admit that many would prefer to date the beginning of the author's mature phase from the next book, *El espejo de agua*, apparently written in its initial form in early 1916. This means that the books, *Ecos del alma* (Echoes of the Soul, 1912), *La gruta del silencio* (The Cavern of Silence, 1913), *Canciones en la noche* (Songs in the Night, 1913) and *Las pagodas ocultas* (Hidden Pagodas, 1914) – all effectively self-published, given that the author paid publishers to issue them – have been excluded, and classified as juvenilia, with the exception of two shaped poems from the third of these volumes, which perhaps offer a little glimpse of things to come, and which have been mentioned in some commentaries as being early *calligrammes*, thus antedating Apollinaire's experiments in this regard. (The latter claim is basically nonsense: shaped poems of this kind, especially with a religious theme, are well-known from classic English poetry, with extant examples including works by Robert Herrick and George Herbert. Rabelais produced at least one in France, and there are even some examples in ancient Greek.)

The main source for the work compiled here is the (mostly) exemplary collected edition of 2003, *Obra poética*, edited by Cedomil Goïc for the UNESCO *Archivos* series. At the time of issuing this *Uncollected*, the UNESCO volume may well be going out of print, given that the entire series is being offered at a substantial discount by the publisher, but it will be worth seeking out after this clearance sale, even at the inflated prices being sought for it in the used-book trade. Some further uncollected poems have been printed in other books in this Shearsman series, especially French versions of poems written in Spanish, or vice-versa, as well as poems that are connected to, or are variants of, other works – our forthcoming edition of *Altazor*, for instance, will present a number of such texts, plus abandoned fragments connected to that project.

I am not going to argue for the literary significance of much of the contents of this *Uncollected* volume, but I do feel that faithful readers of Huidobro's work need to be aware of some of the other things he got up to. As a man living through two world wars and the febrile inter-war years, a period which saw the destruction of a number of empires, and the near-bankruptcy of the major war combatants – barring of course, the USA – it is not surprising that Huidobro jumped into the fray verbally, with hymns in praise of Lenin and the USSR, sorrowful elegies for France and Spain, not to mention his virulent verbal attack on Italian air-force pilots at work in Chile. One may perhaps be forgiven a wry smile at the notion of this aristocrat, living off a private income, being a committed communist.

His astonishing declaration of love for Ximena Amunátegui in the poem, 'Passion, Passion and Death', scandalously published on Good Friday in a national newspaper – the literary editor of which, novelist Juan Emar, was a close friend – is also here, a written expression of that startling *coup de foudre* which altered his life forever. This poem has also been the subject of at least one literary attack, by Enrique Lihn (1929–1988), a significant Chilean poet of the post-war period. Lihn argued that Huidobro's poem had been plagiarised from a long poem, 'Les Pâques à New-York' by the Swiss-French poet, Blaise Cendrars.[1] I find the accusation overblown, but I

[1] The poem was published by Cendrars' own small press in Paris in 1912, but was reprinted in the Paris magazine *La Rose Rouge* in 1919 – where Huidobro is most likely to have seen it – and again, in an illustrated edition, in Paris in 1926.

do think it quite likely that Huidobro took some inspiration from Cendrars' similar address, or prayer, to the Lord, at least as far as form goes. Huidobro would have known Cendrars well enough from their time in Paris, and would have been familiar with the poem. A strange, and perhaps irrelevant, ancillary fact is that, for some time, Cendrars had a wealthy Chilean patron in Paris, a supporter of modern art by name of Eugenia Huici Arguedas de Errázuriz (1860–1951), to whom he had been introduced by Cocteau. I have seen no mention of Sra Errázuriz in biographical descriptions of Huidobro's time in France, but it must be admitted that she had relocated to Biarritz before Huidobro's arrival in Paris; still, it would be fun to speculate on conversations between two upper-class Chilean fans of modern art, both from wine-producing family estates – Errázuriz Panquehue (known simply as Errázuriz outside Chile) on the one hand, and Santa Rita in the case of the Huidobro family – notwithstanding the fact that they stemmed from different generations.

As far as Huidobro was concerned, this poem was not an important part of his literary output, being a *sui generis* explosion aimed at an audience of one, but published in a national newspaper on Good Friday, and thus also intended to shock everyone else. As may be imagined, his wife, Manuela, did not take it at all well, and nor did the rest of his family, her family, or the Amunátegui family. The poem was not collected by the author within the covers of a book during his lifetime, other than in the 1945 *Antología* edited by Eduardo Anguita; one presumes that Anguita, a close friend and supporter, would have cleared this with Huidobro when preparing the book. Huidobro thus did not take it seriously as part of the corpus of his work, but likewise – probably for biographical reasons, following the collapse of his relationship with Ximena shortly before the *Antología* was put together – did not disown it.

Finally, and most significantly, I have included a poem that has been very hard to find anywhere, and which was long thought never to have been published at all. It appears that Huidobro wrote his 'Canto a Lindbergh' just after the famous flight of the *Spirit of St Louis*, while he was based in New York. He then seems to have translated it into English himself, which would account for some errors and clumsy phrasing in the English text.[2] One typescript of the translation has recently been scanned

[2] I say "seems" to have been translated by the author, as we have no proof that he did this on his own. We have no other text in English by Huidobro, but it would appear that he had *some* knowledge of the language. I suspect that he had help, however.

and made available online[3] by the Universidad Católica de Chile, which has acquired an extensive archive of the poet's papers from the Huidobro family foundation. The translation has never been included in the various editions of the author's complete works, and, to my knowledge, its only previous publication was in the special triple number of the Madrid journal *Poesía* (1989) dedicated to Huidobro's life and work, and edited by René de Costa, doyen of Huidobro scholars. There, illegible thumbnail photos of the typescript were accompanied by a Spanish translation of the English text by the editor himself. While obtaining permission to publish this scanned typescript in the present volume, it was a splendid surprise to learn of a variant version of the translation in a cleaner copy, which we are pleased to be able to add here. There appears to be no surviving manuscript of the original Spanish text, but the Cuban poet, Pedro Marqués de Armas, has unearthed a printed version from the pages of Havana's *Diario de la Marina*, where it was published in July 1927, and this text – crucially – differs substantially from the two English typescripts, being somewhat longer and differing at times in its lineation.

Given that the work, in either language, is unfamiliar to almost all readers of Huidobro and has never previously appeared within the covers of a book, I have gone a little overboard in this edition, presenting facsimiles of the originals, together with transcriptions thereof, plus a subsequent reprinting of the Spanish text facing my own translation. This version hews closely to the author's own wherever I think it preferable to do so, but steers away from it when I feel that it is better served by a change, or where I feel that the author's version does not help its own cause. Those readers who prefer the author's version can safely ignore mine, but those who have no Spanish may well find a comparison of the two versions to be instructive. More extensive details are offered in the Appendix to this volume.

Tony Frazer
March, 2025

[3] https://archivospatrimoniales.uc.cl///handle/123456789/61274

ANTES DE 1916

BEFORE 1916

TRIÁNGULO ARMÓNICO

Thesa
La bella
Gentil princesa
Es una blanca estrella
Es una estrella japonesa.
Thesa es la más divina flor de Kioto
Y cuando pasa triunfante en su palanquín
Parece un tierno lirio, parece un pálido loto
Arrancando una tarde de estío del imperial jardín.
Todos la adoran como una diosa, todos hasta el Mikado
Pero ella cruza por entre todos indiferente
De nadie sabe que haya su amor malogrado
Y siempre está risueña, está sonriente.
Es una Ofelia japonesa
Que a las flores amante
Loca y traviesa
Triunfante
Besa.

HARMONIC TRIANGLE

Tissa
Beautiful
Sweet princess
She is a white star
She is a Japanese star
Tissa is Kyoto's most divine bloom
And as she passes triumphantly in her palanquin
She resembles a tender lily, resembles a pale lotus
Plucking a summer evening from the imperial garden.
Everyone adores her like a goddess, everyone, even the Mikado.
But she passes amongst them all with indifference
With no-one knowing of her ill-starred love affair
And she is always merry, always smiling.
She is a Japanese Ophelia
Who is a lover of flowers
Crazy and restless
Triumphant
She is a kisser.

LA CAPILLA ALDEANA

Ave
Canta
suave
que tu canto encanta
sobre el campo inerte
sones
vierte
y ora-
ciones
llora
Desde
la cruz santa
el triunfo del sol canta
y bajo el palio azul del cielo
deshoja tus cantares sobre el suelo
Une tus notas a las de la campana
Que ya se despereza ebria de mañana
Evangelizando la gran quietud aldeana.
Es un amanecer en que una bondad brilla
La capilla está ante la paz de la montaña
Como una limosnera está ante una capilla.
Se esparce en el paisaje el aire de una extraña
Santidad, algo bíblico, algo de piel de oveja
Algo como un rocío lleno de bendiciones
Cual si el campo rezara una idílica queja
Llena de sus caricias y de sus emociones.
La capilla es como una viejita acurrucada
Y al pié de la montaña parece un cuento de Hada
Junto a ella como una bandada de mendigos
Se agrupan y se acercan unos cuantos castaños
Que se asoman curiosos por todos los postigos
Con la malevolencia de los viejos huraños.
Y en el cuadrito lleno de ambiente y de frescura
En el paisaje alegre con castidad de lino
Pinta un brochazo negro la sotana del cura
Cuando ya la tarde alarga su sombra sobre el camino
Parece que se metiera al fondo de la capilla
Y la luz de la gran lámpara con su brillo mortecino
Pinta en la muralla blanca, como una raya amarilla.
Las tablas viejas roncan, crugen, cuando entra el viento oliendo a rosas
Resonga triste en un murmullo el eco santo del rosario
La obscuridad va amalgando y confundiendo así las cosas
Y vuela un «Ángelus» lloroso con lentitud del campanario.

THE VILLAGE CHAPEL

Hail
Sing
softly
so your chant enchants
above the inert field
sounds
pour
out and
prayers
weep
From
the holy cross
the triumph of the sun sings
and under the sky's blue canopy
sheds your songs upon the ground
Join your notes to those of the bell
That wakes up drunk in the morning
Evangelising the village's great tranquillity.
It is a dawn in which a kindness shines out
The chapel stands before the mountain's peace
As a beggar-girl stands before a chapel.
There spreads across the land an air of strange
Sanctity, as if biblical, something like sheepskin
Something like a dew filled with blessings
As if the field were praying an idyllic complaint
Filled with its caresses and its emotions.
The chapel is like an old woman curled up
And at the mountain foot a fairy tale appears
Next to her like a pack of beggars
A few chestnut trees gather and come closer
Peeping curiously through all the shutters
With the malevolence of unsociable old men.
And in the fresh and atmospheric square
On the cheerful landscape with linen celibacy
Paints a black stroke on the priest's cassock
When the evening's shadow lengthens over the road
It appears to be going deep inside the chapel
And the light from the great lamp with its fading glow
Colours onto the white wall, like a yellow stripe.
Old boards snore, creak, as the wind enters, smelling of roses
The sacred echo of the rosary resounds sadly in a murmur.
Darkness keeps on gathering and confusing things this way
And a tearful "Angelus" flies slowly from the bell tower.

POEMAS INÉDITOS

1914–1916

UNCOLLECTED POEMS

1914–1916

VAGUEDAD SUBCONSCIENTE

Pienso en las caras amadas que se han muerto
Caras que mis ojos no verán ya nunca...
¿Quién entra por las puertas que se abren solas?
¿Quién hace crujir los muebles y cambiar las posturas?

Amigos: contadme todas vuestras quimeras muertas,
Decidme de las tardes que llevan al silencio,
Habladme de las frentes que llegan más allá,
Del fondo del espejo que es clepsidra del tiempo.
Yo pensaré en los versos que no haré jamás.

Vuestros brazos hieden a mujeres desnudas
Tenéis en los ojos el paganismo heleno.
Vuestro cansancio duerme en las ojeras lívidas
Y lleváis en los labios un recuerdo obscuro.

Amigos: Nunca en la noche habéis sentido
Al ser que quiere tomar vida
Y se desliza azorado como un niño perdido?...
Yo amo mucho a los hijos que no he tenido
¿Por qué pasé el umbral que trae a la desdicha?

Tengo una vaga obsesión subconsciente
Me siento entrar en los misterios de repente.
El silencio se puebla de una voz insonora
El instante se duerme en el espejo
Que se hace camino para llevarme lejos
Y me siento nadando en una gran luz incolora.

Yo surcaré la sombra para hablar contigo
Y el silencio se cuajará de caras olvidadas
Oh, cuántos ojos muertos mirarán
El dolor de mis sauces en el alma

SUBCONSCIOUS VAGUENESS

I think of the beloved faces that have passed away
Faces that my eyes will never see again…
Who enters through the doors that open by themselves?
Who makes the furniture creak and postures change?

Friends: tell me of all your dead dreams,
Talk to me of the evenings that lead to silence,
Speak to me of brows that reach beyond,
Of the depths of the mirror that is time's clepsydra.
I will think of the verses I will never write.

Your arms reek of naked women
Your eyes hold the paganism of Greece.
Your exhaustion sleeps in livid rings under your eyes
And your lips bear a dark memory.

Friends: at night have you never felt
As if you were a being wanting to come to life
And flitting away in fear like a lost child?…
I dearly love the children I never had
Why did I cross the threshold that brings misfortune?

I have a vague subconscious obsession
I feel myself entering the mysteries all of a sudden.
The silence is filled with a soundless voice
The moment falls asleep in the mirror
That is making its way to carry me off
And I feel as if I am swimming in a great colourless light.

I will plough through the shadows to talk to you
And the silence will fill with forgotten faces
Oh, how many dead eyes will observe
The sorrow of the willows in my soul

Más allá de la vida, más allá del abismo
Se verán los poetas muertos y los que no han nacido
Poetas: Adorad complacientes al Misterio…
¿Quién entra por las puertas que abre el viento?

Beyond life, beyond the abyss
Dead poets will be seen, and poets yet unborn
Poets: yield and worship the Mystery…
Who enters through the doors that the wind opens?

EL PAISAJE SENCILLO

El campo está sereno. Emanan de los pastos
bendiciones al aire, al cielo, a todo…
El paisaje se siente espiritual,
el campo está sencillo como alma de zagal,
no hay tristeza amarilla, no hay nubarrón, no hay lodo.

El castaño levanta sus ramas tercamente
y las alarga en medio de la llanura verde
tanteando en el espacio y el silencio
como un abuelo ciego.

El campo tiene santidad de heno,
de leche y miel, vellón de oveja y de pan bueno,
y de los bueyes la nariz humeante
inciensa de olor bíblico el paisaje.

El campo en la mañana ríe como un pastor,
el sol todo barniza de amarillo decoro
como un gran rey magnánimo, lleno de noble amor,
que arrojara a su pueblo monedas de oro.

Los árboles se llenan de elegante donaire,
sienten correr la savia sana entre sus venas;
ellos no tienen pena:
nunca les falta el agua, el sol, ni el aire.

El camino se extiende como una espalda,
el camino paciente y generoso
que hace el bien sin saberlo,
y a todos lleva a donde quieren ir, gustoso.

El campo tiene castidades de patriarca,
se alza la montaña como un alma

SIMPLE LANDSCAPE

The countryside is calm. From the pastures come
blessings for the air, for the sky, for all…
The landscape feels spiritual,
the countryside as natural as the soul of a shepherd boy;
there is no yellow sadness, no storm cloud, no mud.

The chestnut tree stubbornly raises its branches
and extends them out over the green plain
groping in space and silence
like a blind grandfather.

The countryside has the sanctity of hay,
of milk and honey, sheep's fleece and good bread,
and the steaming nostrils of oxen
incense the landscape with a biblical fragrance.

In the morning the countryside laughs like a shepherd,
the sun varnishes it all with yellow grace
like a great and magnanimous king, full of noble love,
throwing gold coins to his people.

The trees are filled with elegant charm,
they feel the healthy sap running through their veins;
they have no cares:
never do they lack water, sun or air.

The road stretches out like a man's back,
the patient and generous road
that does good without realising it,
and takes everyone where they wish to go, gladly.

The countryside has the chastity of a patriarch.
The mountain rises up like a soul

que se ofreciera toda.
Aquí llora el remanso que al mismo cielo copia,

allá se yergue el rancho oliente a rosas
y a humo viejo,
y más allá el castaño, inmóvil y sereno
que levanta su paz de abuelo ciego.

La tarde llena el campo de Silencio y de Sombra
y reza de rodillas en la montaña;
es la hora en que la carne se pone hosca,
y el alma se pone vaga.

Pasa el agua arrastrando su azul escalofrío
y el sauce que se inclina y se dobla hacia el agua
es como una mujer que en la mañana
fuera a lavar su cabellera al río.

offering itself entirely.
Here weeps the pond reflecting the sky,

there stands the farmhouse smelling of roses
and of old smoke,
and further on the chestnut tree, unmoving and serene
lifting its peace like a blind grandfather.

The afternoon fills the land with Silence and Shadow
kneeling in prayer on the mountain;
it is the time when flesh darkens,
and souls fill with gloom.

Water flows by dragging its blue shiver
and the willow bends, dipping towards the water
like a woman in the morning
washing her hair in the river.

REFINAMIENTO ESPIRITUAL

En mi refinamiento espiritual he llegado a tal punto
que hasta lo más pequeño en mi alma repercute
la esencia de las cosas, el átomo más oculto;
por eso no me entiende quien como yo no ausculte.

Yo escucho cómo late el mochuelo en su huevo
siento el fluido amigo que se acerca,
oigo la noche, siento el crujido de los muertos
y el ruido natural de cada estrella.

Oigo crecer los árboles oigo correr su savia
y escucho cómo ahondan sus raíces en la tierra;
siento el escarabajo que se arrastra
y la agonía de los lirios que se quiebran.

Escucho el pensamiento del amigo malo
que medita en la sombra una venganza
y veo que en lo negro se suicida algo blanco,
y la sorpresa que llega con sigilo de gata.

El ruido más sutil, el roce más prudente:
calofrío en el musgo, figura que resbala,
la sombra que se escurre, el ala más lejana
lo que nadie adivina, lo que nadie presiente
en mi espíritu toma vibración de campanas.

Y con constancia de hormiga
mis sentidos muy atentos,
acarrean por los ojos
cosas nuevas al cerebro.

¡Oh! Santas Hormiguitas
que a mi Pagoda Oculta
lleváis vuestra semilla
paciente que fecunda.

SPIRITUAL REFINEMENT

In my spiritual refinement I have reached the point
where even the smallest thing resonates in my soul
the essence of all things, the most hidden atom;
that is why no understands me who does not probe as I do.

I hear the owl's heartbeat inside the egg
I sense the friendly current approaching,
I hear the night, I sense the creaking of the dead
and the natural sound of every star.

I hear the trees growing I hear their sap flowing
I hear their roots burrowing deep into the earth;
I feel the beetle crawling along
and the death throes of broken lilies.

I hear the thoughts of a wicked friend
brooding in the shadows on revenge
and I see something white in the darkness killing itself,
and the surprise creeping in with the stealth of a cat.

The subtlest noise, the gentlest touch:
shivers in the moss, a figure slipping away,
the shadow that escapes, the farthest wing
what no one foresees, what no one senses
takes on the vibration of bells in my spirit.

And with the constancy of an ant
my senses ever alert,
gather through my eyes
new things for the mind.

Oh! You Blessed Ants
who carry your seeds
patient and fertile
to my Hidden Pagoda.

OCASO EN EL ESPEJO

En el jardín y en el espejo
Caen las hojas de los árboles
En el jardín y en el espejo
Se van las horas por la tarde

El jardín se sabe duplicado
Por el divino mago
Y aumenta sus encantos

Por el espejo y el Ocaso
Ha cruzado un pájaro

Y este mago cristal
Se me hace un arroyuelo
Y se alarga indefinidamente
Para dar a mis pies atracciones de senderos

En el espejo acuoso muriendo va la tarde
En una despedida interminable.

SUNSET IN THE MIRROR

In the garden and in the mirror
Leaves fall from the trees
In the garden and in the mirror
The hours drift away with the evening

The garden knows it has been duplicated
By the divine sorcerer
And increases its enchantments

A bird has crossed
Through the mirror and the Sunset

And this crystal sorcerer
Becomes a rivulet for me
And it goes on indefinitely
Offering my feet the allure of trails

In the watery mirror the evening fades away
In a never-ending farewell.

[SIN TITULO]

Una poesía que haga sentir la
pureza del hombre
Algo fuera del tiempo
Hay que crear un mundo que pueda
satisfacer a los verdaderos poetas
Los bellos poemas se escriben
mañana
Hay que llevar entre los cabellos
un cielo estrellado y una tierra perfecta.
Escribir esos poemas que irritan a
los mediocres porque les hacen sentir
ver las distancias
Cosas que se imponen por su
pureza, por su altura por su
grandeza.
Sed sobrios. No hay nada más terrible
que el rastacuerismo en el arte.

[UNTITLED]

A poetry that makes one feel the
purity of mankind
Something out of time
We must create a world that can
satisfy true poets
The most beautiful poems will be written
tomorrow
We must wear in our hair
a starry sky and a perfect earth.
Writing those poems that irritate
mediocrities because they make them have feelings
see into the distance
Things imposed by their
purity, by their height by their
greatness.
Be sober. There is nothing more terrible
than pomposity in art.

EL HIJO PRÓDIGO

Muchacho
Muchacho
Tienes el brazo demasiado corto para boxear con Dios
Pero Jesús ha dicho una parábola:
Cierto hombre tenía dos hijos,
Jesús no nos ha dicho cómo se llamaba ese hombre
Ni tampoco nos ha dicho el nombre de sus hijos.
Pero todo joven
En todas partes
Es uno de esos dos hijos.

Y el más joven dijo a su padre:
Divide nuestro patrimonio y dame pronto
La parte que me toca.
Y el padre, con lágrimas en los ojos le dijo:
Hijo mío, no abandones la casa de tu padre.
Pero ese hijo estaba lleno de orgullo
Y de voluntad,
Y cogió su parte en los bienes de su padre
Y partió para lejanos países.

Llega un día
Llega siempre una hora
En la cual todo joven
Desde lo alto de la casa paterna
Contempla el horizonte
Y sueña en lejanos viajes.

Y el hijo pródigo
Caminó por rutas desconocidas
Y mientras andaba iba pensando:
Héme aquí sobre una ruta fácil
Y dulce y lisa,

THE PRODIGAL SON

Young man
Young man
Your arms are too short to box with God
But Jesus told a parable:
There was a man who had two sons;
Jesus did not tell us that man's name
Nor did He tell us the names of his sons.
But every youth
Wherever he might be
Is one of those two sons.

And the younger said to his father:
Divide our inheritance and give me now
The part that is mine.
And the father, with tears in his eyes, said to him:
My son, do not forsake your father's house.
But that son was filled with pride
And determination,
And he took his share of his father's wealth
And left for distant lands.

There comes the day
Always there comes the time
When every young man
Gazes at the horizon
From the top of his father's house
And dreams of distant journeys.

And the prodigal son
Went along unknown roads
And as he walked he thought:
Here I am on an easy road
Smooth and gentle,

Muy lejos de los surcos disparejos
Tras los arados de mi padre.

Muchacho, muchacho
Es muy fácil de seguir la ruta
Que conduce al Infierno
Va siempre de bajada,
Y mientras más se avanza más rápido se va.
No hay que padecer ni sudar ni empujar,
Sólo dejarse ir, flotar, resbalar
Hasta el momento que los pies hacen resonar
Con espantoso choque las puertas del infierno.

Y el hijo pródigo siguió su camino.
Y una tarde llegó a una ciudad inmensa
La cual brillaba de tantos fuegos
Que la noche se parecía al día.
Las calles estaban llenas de gente,
Se oían por todas partes los cobres y las cuerdas
De mil orquestas,
Y en todas las calles cantaban, reían, bailaban.
Y el hijo pródigo se acercó a un transeúnte:
Decidme ¿qué ciudad es ésta?
Y el transeúnte se puso a reír y le dijo:
Es Babilonia, Babilonia.
La gran ciudad de Babilonia.
Venid, amigo, venid con nosotros.
Y el hijo pródigo se unió a la multitud.

Muchacho, muchacho
Nunca se está solo en Babilonia,
Siempre encontrarás amigos en Babilonia
Muchacho, muchacho
Nunca puedes estar solo en Babilonia

Nunca estar solo con tu Jesús en Babilonia
Jamás se puede encontrar un sitio desierto,

Far away from the uneven furrows
Behind my father's plough.

Young man, young man
It is very easy to follow the road
That leads to Hell
It always goes downhill,
And the further you travel, the faster you go.
There is no need to suffer or sweat or push,
Just let yourself go, floating, sliding along
Until the moment your feet crash
Against the gates of Hell making a frightful echo.

And the prodigal son continued on his way.
One evening he arrived at a huge city
Which glowed with so many fires
That night seemed like day.
The streets were full of people,
Everywhere one could hear the brass and strings
Of a thousand orchestras,
And in every street there was singing, laughter, dancing.
And the prodigal son approached a passer-by:
Tell me, what city is this?
And the passer-by laughed and said to him:
This is Babylon, Babylon.
The great city of Babylon.
Come, my friend, come with us.
And the prodigal son joined the crowd.

Young man, young man
You are never alone in Babylon,
You will always find friends in Babylon
Young man, young man
You can never be alone in Babylon

You will never be alone with your Jesus in Babylon
You will never find a deserted place,

Ni un lugar tranquilo para poner tus dos rodillas
Y hablar con vuestro Dios en Babilonia.

Y el hijo pródigo siguió a su nuevo amigo,
Se compró hermosos trajes nuevos.
Pasó sus días en las tabernas
Bebiendo todos los fuegos del Infierno.
Pasó todas sus noches en los garitos,
Jugando su alma a los dados con el diablo.

Encontró las mujeres de Babilonia
¡Oh! ¡Oh! ¡Esas mujeres de Babilonia!
Vestidas de amarillo, de púrpura y de escarlata
Cargadas de anillos, pendientes y brazaletes.
Sus labios chorrean una miel sabrosa
Que perfuma a jazmín.

Y ese olor de jazmín de las mujeres de Babilonia
Entró en sus narices y penetró su alma.
Y malbarató la esencia de su vida en las orgías,
En las noches negras con las mujeres de Babilonia
Con esas mujeres cuyos pecados tiene la dulzura del almíbar.
Ellas le robaron su plata, le robaron sus ropas
Y lo dejaron sin un céntimo, en harapos
En las calles de Babilonia.

Entonces el hijo pródigo se enroló
En otra multitud
La de los mendigos y los leprosos de Babilonia.

Y tuvo que alimentar a los puercos
Y tenía más hambre que los puercos
Y se acostó sobre su vientre en el estiércol y en el barro,

Y comió los restos de los cerdos,
Y ningún cerdo era tan vil como para volver su hocico
Hacia el hombre que arrastraba en el barro de Babilonia.

Nor a quiet place to kneel
And speak with your God in Babylon.

And the prodigal son followed his new friend,
Bought himself fine new clothes.
He spent his days in taverns
Drinking all the fires of Hell.
He spent his nights in gambling dens,
Wagering his soul with the devil's dice.

He met the women of Babylon
Oh! Oh! Those women of Babylon!
Dressed in yellow, purple and scarlet
Loaded with rings, pendants and bracelets.
Their lips dripped with delicious honey
Scented with jasmine.

And that jasmine scent of the women of Babylon
Entered his nostrils and penetrated his soul.
And he squandered the essence of his life in orgies,
On black nights with the women of Babylon
With those women whose sins have the sweetness of syrup.
They stole his money, they stole his clothes.
And they left him penniless, in rags
On the streets of Babylon.

Then the prodigal son joined up
With another crowd
That of the beggars and lepers of Babylon.

And he had to feed the pigs
And he was hungrier than the pigs
And he lay on his belly in the dung and the mud,

          And he ate the pigs' scraps,
And no pig was so vile as to turn its snout
Towards the man who crawled in the mud of Babylon.

Un día el hijo pródigo reflexionó y pensó:
En la casa de mi padre hay cuartos y cuartos
Y todos los servidores comen a su antojo,
Y todos tienen un lecho para dormir.
Voy a levantarme y volveré a casa de mi padre.

Y su padre le vio venir desde lejos
Y le cubrió de ropas limpias
Y le colgó al cuello una cadena de oro.
Y le colgó al cuello una cadena de oro.
Hizo preparar una gran festín,
Mató al ternero más gordo e invitó a todos sus vecinos.

¡Oh! ¡Oh! pecador
Cuando te mezclas con las muchedumbres de Babilonia,
Cuando bebes el vino de Babilonia,
Cuando persigues a las mujeres de Babilonia,
Ríes a la faz de Dios y olvidas la Muerte.
Hoy día, muchacho,
Tienes en tu brazo la fuerza de un oso
Y en tu cuello la fuerza de un toro.
Pero uno de estos días
Tendrás que batirte con la muerte
Y la muerte ganará.

Muchacho, no te acerques a Babilonia
Babilonia está en las bocas del infierno.
Muchacho abandona las danzas y las orgías.

Y el vino y el whisky
Y la boca quemante de las mujeres de Babilonia
Arrójate de rodillas y exclama en el fondo de tu corazón:
Quiero levantarme y volver a casa de mi padre.

Tienes en tu brazo la fuerza de un oso
Y en tu cuello la fuerza de un toro,
Pero uno de estos días

One day the prodigal son reflected and thought:
In my father's house there are so many rooms
And all the servants eat as they please,
And everyone has a bed to sleep in.
I will get up and return to my father's house.

And his father saw him coming from afar
And clothed him with clean garments
And hung a gold chain around his neck.
And hung a gold chain around his neck.
He had a great feast prepared,
Slaughtered the fattest calf and invited all his neighbours.

Oh! Oh! sinner
When you mingle with the crowds of Babylon,
When you drink the wine of Babylon,
When you pursue the women of Babylon,
You laugh in the face of God and you forget Death.
Today, young man,
Your arm has the strength of a bear
And your neck the strength of a bull.
But one of these days
You will have to wrestle with death
And death will win.

Young man, do not go near Babylon.
Babylon lies in the jaws of Hell.
Young man, abandon the dances and orgies.

And the wine and the whisky
And the burning mouths of the women of Babylon
Fall to your knees and cry out from the depths of your heart:
I will rise up and return to my father's house.

Your arm has the strength of a bear
And your neck the strength of a bull,
But one of these days

Tendrás que batirte con la muerte.
Y la muerte ganará.

Muchacho, no te acerques a Babilonia
Babilonia está en las bocas del Infierno.
Muchacho abandona las danzas y las orgías.

Y el vino y el whisky
Y la boca quemante de las mujeres de Babilonia
Arrójate de rodillas y exclama en el fondo de tu corazón:
Quiero levantarme y volver a casa de mi padre.

You will wrestle with death.
And death will win.

Young man, do not go near Babylon.
Babylon lies in the jaws of Hell.
Young man, abandon the dances and orgies.

And the wine and the whisky
And the burning mouths of the women of Babylon
Fall to your knees and cry out from the depths of your heart:
I will rise up and return to my father's house.

CANTO A LINDBERGH

CANTO TO LINDBERGH

Canto a Lindberg

De las manos ilustres de D. Gonzalo Aróstegui hemos recibido la presente composición del notable poeta y crítico chileno D. Vicente García Huidobro. Agradecemos a tan distinguido amigo el gentil envío, en nombre de nuestros lectores.

Como una serpentina lanzada de New York a París
Atraviesas el cielo del Atlántico, y todo el cielo gris
Se llena de tu risa. Tu sonrisa con las alas abiertas
Avanzando por las rutas inciertas.

Las olas se levantan y te miran,
Y tú pasas lejos como el amanecer.
Las montañas llegan al fondo y viran,
Las naciones desfilan hacia ayer.

Despreocupado, alegre
Te juegas la vida entre dos estrellas,
Que te tienden las manos para cuidar tu vida.
Tú filialmente te confías a ellas,
Porque sabes que el infinito te ama,
Que eres el regalón del cielo y de los elementos.
Y sientes que el espacio te acaricia y te llama
Por tu propio nombre, familiar a los vientos.

Tu ruta quedará en la historia del mundo
Como un arco iris entre América y Francia,
Como un lazo invisible de sonido y fragancia,
Pero más fuerte que todos, más vital y profundo.

Bajo ese arco de triunfo pasarán los siglos en su
(marcha eterna,
Bajo ese arco de triunfo rugirán las olas su sonata
(interna,
Bajo ese arco de triunfo cantarán los barcos su can-
(ción moderna.

Los hombres dormían como un ejército cansado
Cuando el aire sintió el cantar de tu hélice y el peso
(de tu motor alado,
Domador de horizontes y destinos,
Misionero de los nuevos caminos
Al saberte en el cielo los pueblos despertaron,
Millones de miradas subieron en una sola oración
Y el mundo se animó como un tambor.

CANTO A LINDBERGH

(Transcripción del texto del periódico / Transcription of the newspaper text)

Como una serpentina lanzada de Nueva York a París
Atraviesas el cielo del Atlántico, y todo el cielo gris
Se llena de tu risa. Tu sonrisa con las alas abiertas
Avanzando por las rutas inciertas.

Las olas se levantan y te miran,
Y tú pasas lejos como el amanecer.
Las montañas llegan al fondo y viran,
Las naciones desfilan hacía ayer.

Despreocupado, alegre
Te juegas la vida entre dos estrellas,
Que te tienden las manos para cuidar tu vida.
Tú filialmente te confías a ellas,
Porque sabes que el infinito te ama,
Que eres el regalón del cielo y de los elementos,
Y sientes que el espacio te acaricia y te llama
Por tu propio nombre, familiar a los vientos.

Tu ruta quedará en la historia del mundo
Como un arco iris entre América y Francia,
Como un lazo invisible de sonido y fragancia,
Pero más fuerte que todos, más vital y profundo.

Bajo ese arco de triunfo pasarán los siglos en su marcha eterna,
Bajo ese arco de triunfo rugirán las olas su sonata interna,
Bajo ese arco de triunfo cantarán los barcos su canción moderna.

Los hombres dormían como un ejército cansado
Cuando el aire sintió el cantar de tu hélice y el peso de tu motor alado,
Domador de horizontes y destinos,
Misionero de los nuevos caminos
Al saberte en el cielo los pueblos despertaron,
Millones de miradas subieron en una sola oración
Y el mundo se animó como un tambor.

Francia, madre de la aviación y de tanta cosa gran-
Te recibe y te aplaude más que nadie. (de,
Ella, que acababa de perder dos hijos en igual an-
Te dice al oído: (helo,
—Hijo mío, que estás en los cielos,
Lleva a mis dos hijos este ramo de rosas de Francia,
y que todo el cielo
Se perfume por un año entero.

Un hurra se propaga
Como cien mil campanas,
Hurra lanzado de abismo en abismo
Entre nubes rocosas y la chispa
Que brota del contacto.
Es el mismo,
El mismo corazón del aire intacto.
La eternidad sobre el naufragio
Y sobre ambos la confianza temblante del ala
inclinada del uno al otro borde del vacío.
Es el mismo. Es la imagen del hombre que en el aire
(resbala,
Lleva sombras ajenas, olor de nuevos astros,
Y como un perro va siguiendo rastros
Por la Vía Láctea.
Es él.
Es el mismo,
Blanco sobre el abismo,
Señor y dueño
Del tiempo y del espacio.
Hermoso. Hermoso
En las marmolerías del sueño.

Tu cabeza en el cielo, el cielo es tu corona de estre-
(llas silenciosas.
Una nube te trae un ramo de rosas
Y tú miras de arriba el pobre globo sembrado de
(cruces,
Este planeta nuestro que pasa en el vacío
Lento, lento y lleno de luces
Como un acorazado siguiendo la carriente de un río.

Francia, madre de la aviación y de tanta cosa grande,
Te recibe y te aplaude más que nadie.
Ella, que acababa de perder dos hijos en igual anhelo,
Te dice al oído:
—Hijo mío, que estás en los cielos,
Lleva a mis dos hijos este ramo de rosas de Francia
y que todo el cielo
Se perfume por un año entero.

Un hurra se propaga
Como cien mil campanas.
Hurra lanzado de abismo en abismo
Entre nubes rocosas y la chispa
Que brota del contacto.
                                        Es el mismo,
El mismo corazón del aire intacto.
La eternidad sobre el naufragio
Y sobre ambos la confianza temblante del ala
Inclinada del uno al otro borde del vacío.
Es el mismo. Es la imagen del hombre que en el aire resbala,
Lleva sombras ajenas, olor de nuevos astros,
Y como un perro va siguiendo rastros
Por la Vía Láctea
   Es él.
            Es el mismo,
Blanco sobre el abismo,
Señor y dueño
Del tiempo y del espacio.
Hermoso. Hermoso
En las marmolerías del sueño.

Tu cabeza en el cielo, el cielo es tu corona de estrellas silenciosas.
Una nube te trae un ramo de rosas
Y tú miras de arriba el pobre globo sembrado de cruces,
Este planeta nuestro que pasa en el vacío
Lento, lento y lleno de luces
Como un acorazado siguiendo la corriente de un río.

La vida. La tierra.
¿Ves? ¡Qué cosa absurda!
Un camello hace el ritmo del desierto,
Un tren que marcha,
Un hombre que piensa,
Una mujer que baila,
Un cementerio lejos como un rebaño muerto
Y un oso solo,
Lamiendo el eje de la tierra en medio del polo.

Hoy vuelves como un cometa con tu manto de
(victoria
Y una bandada de aplausos agita sus alas y vuela
(hacia tu gloria.
El cielo está bordado de tu nombre
Y como en un día de fiesta se ha llenado de encajes.
Niño imprudente, tenías poco más de veinte años
(de sonrisas
Y eras alegre como una isla después de un largo viaje.
Ahora tendrás que soportar la seriedad de cien mi-
(llones de hombres.

Pero no importa, porque tu acto
Hace todo más puro, hace todo más alto,
Eleva las montañas, eleva las llanuras
(Las cordilleras tienen mil metros más),
Levanta el entusiasmo de las almas más duras.

Y por eso en mi lengua española,
En mi lengua que tiene balanceos de ola;
La lengua que se hablaba en las tres carabelas
Que encontraron la tierra donde viste la luz,
Te saludo y te canto. Me recuerda tu hazaña
La historia de mi raza, las proezas de España.

Vicente García Huidobro

El texto editorial al comienzo del poema dice:

De las manos ilustres de D. Gonzalo Aróstegui hemos recibido la presente composición del notable poeta y crítico chileno D. Vicente García Huidobro. Agradecemos a tan distinguido amigo el gentil envío, en nombre de nuestros lectores.

La vida. La tierra.
¿Ves? ¡Qué cosa absurda!
Un camello hace el ritmo del desierto,
Un tren que marcha,
Un hombre que piensa,
Una mujer que baila,
Un cementerio lejos como un rebaño muerto
Y un oso solo,
Lamiendo el eje de la tierra en medio del polo.

Hoy vuelves como un cometa con tu manto de victoria
Y una bandada de aplausos agita sus alas y vuela hacia tu gloria.
El cielo está bordado de tu nombre
Y como en un día de fiesta se ha llenado de encajes.
Niño imprudente, tenías poco más de veinte años de sonrisas
Y eras alegre como una isla después de un largo viaje.
Ahora tendrás que soportar la seriedad de cien mil millones de hombres.

Pero no importa, porque tu acto
Hace todo más puro, hace todo más alto,
Eleva las montañas, eleva las llanuras
(Las cordilleras tienen mil metros más),
Levanta el entusiasmo de las almas más duras.

Y por eso en mi lengua española,
En mi lengua que tiene balanceos de ola;
La lengua que se hablaba en las tres carabelas
Que encontraron la tierra donde viste la luz,
Te saludo y te canto. Me recuerda tu hazaña
La historia de mi raza, las proezas de España.

The editorial text at the head of the poem reads:

From the illustrious hands of Don Gonzalo Aróstegui we have received this composition by the noted Chilean poet and critic, Don Vicente García Huidobro. On behalf of our readers, we express our thanks to such a distinguished friend for having sent it to us.

Vicente Huidobro.

02982
MS 357
(1-7)

CANTO TO LINDBERGH

translated from the Spanish

Like a spiral hurled from New York to Paris,
You travelled the sky of the Atlantic, the grey sky
Was filled with your smile-- your smile of opened wings
Advancing on uncertain routes.
The waves stand up to see you, and you pass
Far away like the dawn breaking.
The mountains approach and girate,
The nations file off toward yesterday.
Your route will stay in the history of the world
Like a rainbow between America and France,
Like an invisible lasso of sound and fragrance,
But stronger than all, more vital and profound.
Below that triumphal arch, the centuries
Will pass in their eternal trudge.
Below that triumphal arch the waves moan their inner sonata.
Below that triumphal arch the ships will sing their modern song.
Men slept like a tired army
When the air felt the singing of your propeller and the weight of your winged motor--

Tamer of horizons and destinies,
Pioneer of new roads.
When the people knew you in the air, they awakened;
Millions of eyes turned upward in one prayer,
And the world was vibrant like a drum.

CANTO TO LINDBERGH (1)

(Transcripción del texto mecanografiado / Transcription of the typescript)
Translation by the author

Like a spiral hurled from New York to Paris,
You travelled the sky of the Atlantic, the grey sky
Was filled with your smile— your smile of opened wings
Advancing on uncertain routes.
The waves stand up to see you, and you pass
Far away like the dawn breaking.
The mountains approach and gyrate,
The nations file off toward yesterday.[1]

Your route will stay in the history of the world
Like a rainbow between America and France,
Like an invisible lasso of sound and fragrance,
But stronger than all, more vital and profound.
Below that triumphal arch, the centuries
Will pass in their eternal trudge.
Below that triumphal arch the waves moan their inner sonata.
Below that triumphal arch the ships will sing their modern song.
Men slept like a tired army
When the air felt the singing of your propeller and the weight of your
[winged motor—
Tamer of horizons and destinies,
Pioneer of new roads.

When the people knew you in the air, they awakened;
Millions of eyes turned upward in one prayer,
And the world was vibrant like a drum.

---

[1] I take the pencil line drawn at the left of the page after this line to be an indication of a stanza break, as in the published Spanish text.

Hurrah! thrown from abyss to abyss

Between clouds of stone, sparks light up, firing from the
contact.

--It is the same,

The same heart of the air intact.

Eternity over the wreck

And over both the trembling confidence of the wings

Inclined from the borders of space.

It is the same, the image of man

Who flutters in the air

Carrying remote shadows, odor of new planets,

And like a dog, goes loping on the Milky Way.

It is he

The same

White over the abyss

Lord and Master

Of time and space.

Beautiful! beautiful!

In the marble work of dreams.

Your head in the sky, the sky your crown

Of silent stars.

A cloud brings you xxxxx a wreath of roses,

And you see from above, the poor globe

Strewn with crosses,

This planet of ours that passes in the void,

Slowly, slowly, and filled with lights

Like a cruiser drifting in the currents of a river.

Life.

Earth.

2

Hurrah! thrown from abyss to abyss
Between clouds of stone, sparks light up, firing from the contact.
—It is the same,
The same heart of the air intact.
Eternity over the wreck
And over both the trembling confidence of the wings
Inclined from the borders of space.
It is the same, the image of man
Who flutters in the air
Carrying remote shadows, odor of new planets,
And like a dog, goes loping on the Milky Way.
It is he
The same
White over the abyss
Lord and Master
Of time and space.
Beautiful! beautiful!
In the marble work of dreams.
Your head in the sky, the sky your crown
Of silent stars.
A cloud brings you a wreath of roses,
And you see from above, the poor globe
Strewn with crosses,
This planet of ours that passes in the void,
Slowly, slowly, and filled with lights
Like a cruiser drifting in the currents of a river.
Life.
Earth.

3

Do you see? What an absurd thing!

A camel makes the rhythm of the desert.

a train speeding
~~An animal that walks~~

A man who thinks

A woman who dances

A faraway cemetary like a dead herd, and a lone bear

Licking the axis of the earth in the middle of the Pole.

Now you return like a comet.

With your mantle of ~~xxxxx~~ victory.

And a flock of applause flutters wings toward your glory.

The heaven is broidered with your name

And like a day of festival, is decked with lace.

Imprudent child, you had only a little more
than twenty years of smiles,

And you were happy, like an island after a long voyage--

Now you must support the seriousness of a hundred million
people.

But no matter, since your deed makes everything purer,
everything higher.

It lifts the mountains, it lifts the plains,

It lifts the enthusiasms of the hardest souls.

And for that, in my Spanish tongue,

In my language that has the roll of waves,

The language spoken ~~xx~~ in the three caravels

That found the land where you saw the light

I salute you and sing to you;

Your deed recalls the history of my race,

The prowess of Spain.

Vicente Huidobro

3

Do you see? What an absurd thing!
A camel makes the rhythm of the desert.
~~An animal that walks~~ A train speeding
A man who thinks
A woman who dances
A faraway cemetery like a dead herd, and a lone bear
Licking the axis of the earth in the middle of the Pole.
Now you return like a comet
With your mantle of victory.
And a flock of applause flutters wings toward your glory.
The heaven is broidered with your name [1]
And like a day of festival, is decked with lace.
Imprudent child, you had only a little more
    than twenty years of smiles,[2]
And you were happy, like an island after a long voyage—
Now you must support the seriousness of a hundred million people.
But no matter, since your deed makes everything purer, everything higher.
It lifts the mountains, it lifts the plains,
It lifts the enthusiasms of the hardest souls.
And for that, in my Spanish tongue,
In my language that has the roll of waves,
The language spoken in the three caravels
That found the land where you saw the light
I salute you and sing to you;
Your deed recalls the history of my race,
The prowess of Spain.

---

[1] This is obviously poor English and should read "The heavens are embroidered with your name".

[2] I believe this line should be one with its predecessor, but the second version of the translation pushes this line to the left margin, with an initial capital.

CANTO TO LINDBERGH

By Vicente Huidobro

(Translated from the Spanish)

Like a spiral hurled from New York to Paris,
You travelled the sky of the Atlantic, the grey sky
Was filled with your smile--your smile of opened wings
Advancing on uncertain routes.
The waves stand up to see you, and you pass
Far away like the dawn breaking.
The mountains approach and gyrate.
The nations file off toward yesterday.
Carefree, happy,
You gamble your life between two stars
That stretch their hands to protect you.
And you like a son have confidence in them,
Because you know that the infinite loves you,
Because you are the spoiled child of the sky and the elements,
And feel that space caresses you and calls you
By your very name, familiar to the winds.

When the air felt the singing of your propeller and the weight of your winged motor--
Tamer of horizons and destinies,
Pioneer of new roads.

CANTO TO LINDBERGH (2)

(Transcripción del texto mecanografiado / Transcription of the typescript)
Translation by the author

Like a spiral hurled from New York to Paris,
You travelled the sky of the Atlantic, the grey sky
Was filled with your smile—your smile of opened wings
Advancing on uncertain routes.
The waves stand up to see you, and you pass
Far away like the dawn breaking.
The mountains approach and gyrate,
The nations file off toward yesterday.
    Carefree, happy,
You gamble your life between two stars
That stretch their hands to protect you.
And you like a son have confidence in them,
Because you know that the infinite loves you,
Because you are the spoiled child of the sky and the elements,
And feel that space caresses you and calls you
By your very name, familiar to the winds.

When the air felt the singing of your propeller and the weight of your
                                        [winged motor—
Tamer of horizons and destinies,
Pioneer of new roads.

Canto to Lindbergh - 2

When the people knew you in the air, they awakened;
Millions of eyes turned upward in one prayer,
And the world was vibrant like a drum.
Hurrah! thrown from abyss to abyss
Between clouds of stone, sparks light up, firing from the contact.
-- it is the same,
The same heart of the air intact.
Eternity over the wreck
And over both the trembling confidence of the wings
Inclined from the borders of space.
It is the same, the image of man
Who flutters in the air
Carrying remote shadows, odor of new planets,
And like a dog, goes loping on the Milky Way.
It is he
The same
White over the abyss
Lord and Master
Of time and space.
Beautiful! beautiful!
In the marble work of dreams.
Your head in the sky, the sky your crown
Of silent stars.
A cloud brings you a wreath of roses,
And you see from above, the poor globe
Strewn with crosses

— 2 —

When the people knew you in the air, they awakened;
Millions of eyes turned upward in one prayer,
And the world was vibrant like a drum.
Hurrah! thrown from abyss to abyss
Between clouds of stone, sparks light up, firing from the contact.
—it is the same,
The same heart of the air intact.
Eternity over the wreck
And over both the trembling confidence of the wings
Inclined from the borders of space.
It is the same, the image of man
Who flutters in the air
Carrying remote shadows, odor of new planets,
And like a dog, goes loping on the Milky Way.
It is he
The same
White over the abyss
Lord and Master
Of time and space.
Beautiful! beautiful!
In the marble work of dreams.
Your head in the sky, the sky your crown
Of silent stars.
A cloud brings you a wreath of roses,
And you see from above, the poor globe
Strewn with crosses

This planet of ours that passes in the void,
Slowly, slowly, and filled with lights
Like a cruiser drifting in the currents of a river.
Life.
Earth.
Do you see? What an absurd thing!
A camel makes the rhythm of the desert.
A train speeding,
A man who thinks,
A woman who dances,
A far away cemetery like a dead herd, and a lone bear
Licking the axis of the earth in the middle of the Pole.
Now you return like a comet
With your mantle of victory,
And a flock of applause flutters wings toward your glory.
The heaven is broidered with your name,
And like a day of festival, is decked with lace.
Imprudent child, you had only a little more
Than twenty years of smiles,
And you were happy, like an island after a long voyage-
Now you must support the seriousness of a hundred million people.
But no matter, since your deed makes everything purer, everything higher.
It lifts the mountains, it lifts the plains,
It lifts the enthusiasms of the hardest souls.
And for that, in my Spanish tongue,
In my language that has the roll of waves,

— 3 —

This planet of ours that passes in the void,
Slowly, slowly, and filled with lights
Like a cruiser drifting in the currents of a river.
    Life.
            Earth.
Do you see? What an absurd thing!
A camel makes the rhythm of the desert.
A train speeding,
A man who thinks,
A woman who dances,
A far away cemetery like a dead herd, and a lone bear
Licking the axis of the earth in the middle of the Pole.
Now you return like a comet
With your mantle of victory.
And a flock of applause flutters wings toward your glory.
The heaven is broidered with your name,[1]
And like a day of festival, is decked with lace.
Imprudent child, you had only a little more
Than twenty years of smiles,
And you were happy, like an island after a long voyage—
Now you must support the seriousness of a hundred million people.
But no matter, since your deed makes everything purer, everything higher.
It lifts the mountains, it lifts the plains,
It lifts the enthusiasms of the hardest souls.
And for that, in my Spanish tongue,
In my language that has the roll of waves,

---

[1] As in the first version, this is obviously poor English and would better read "The heavens are embroidered with your name".

Canto to Lindbergh - 4

The language spoken in the three caravels
That found the land where you saw the light,
I salute you and sing to you;
Your deed recalls the history of my race,
The prowess of Spain.

Vicente Huidobro

— 4 —

The language spoken in the three caravels
That found the land where you saw the light.
I salute you and sing to you;
Your deed recalls the history of my race,
The prowess of Spain.

CANTO A LINDBERGH

Como una serpentina lanzada de Nueva York a París
Atraviesas el cielo del Atlántico, y todo el cielo gris
Se llena de tu risa. Tu sonrisa con las alas abiertas
Avanzando por las rutas inciertas.

Las olas se levantan y te miran,
Y tú pasas lejos como el amanecer.
Las montañas llegan al fondo y viran,
Las naciones desfilan hacía ayer.

Despreocupado, alegre
Te juegas la vida entre dos estrellas,
Que te tienden las manos para cuidar tu vida.
Tú filialmente te confías a ellas,
Porque sabes que el infinito te ama,
Que eres el regalón del cielo y de los elementos,
Y sientes que el espacio te acaricia y te llama
Por tu propio nombre, familiar a los vientos.

Tu ruta quedará en la historia del mundo
Como un arco iris entre América y Francia,
Como un lazo invisible de sonido y fragancia,
Pero más fuerte que todos, más vital y profundo.

Bajo ese arco de triunfo pasarán los siglos en su marcha eterna,
Bajo ese arco de triunfo rugirán las olas su sonata interna,
Bajo ese arco de triunfo cantarán los barcos su canción moderna.

SONG FOR LINDBERGH[1]

translated by Tony Frazer

Like a spiral hurled from New York to Paris
You crossed the Atlantic sky, and the entire grey sky
Is filled with your laughter. Your smile with its wings spread
Advancing along uncertain routes.

The waves rise up and watch you,
And you fade away like the dawn.
The mountains recede into the background and turn,[2]
The nations march off towards yesterday.

Carefree, happy
You gamble with your life between two stars,
That hold their hands out to protect your life.
You entrust yourself to them like a son,
Because you know that infinity loves you,
That you are the youngest of the heavens and the elements,
And you feel that space caresses you and calls you
By your own name, familiar to the winds.

Your route will remain in the history of the world
Like a rainbow between America and France,
Like an invisible lasso of sound and fragrance,
But stronger than all, more vital and profound.

Beneath that triumphal arch centuries will pass on their eternal march,
Beneath that triumphal arch waves will moan their inner sonata,
Beneath that triumphal arch ships will sing their modern song.

---

[1] The author's English title (see pp56-7 and 62-63) is a word-for-word translation of the Spanish, but is unidiomatic. The Spanish title could be translated as 'Song for…', 'Song to…', 'Canto for/to…' or even as 'I Sing to…'.

[2] My version here is very different from the author's. His translation does not account for *al fondo*. Likewise, his "gyrate" would be a translation of *girar* rather than *virar*, which suggests that the Spanish text might have existed in another version.

Los hombres dormían como un ejército cansado
Cuando el aire sintió el cantar de tu hélice y el peso de tu motor alado,
Domador de horizontes y destinos,
Misionero de los nuevos caminos
Al saberte en el cielo los pueblos despertaron,
Millones de miradas subieron en una sola oración
Y el mundo se animó como un tambor.

Francia, madre de la aviación y de tanta cosa grande,
Te recibe y te aplaude más que nadie.
Ella, que acababa de perder dos hijos en igual anhelo,
Te dice al oído:
—Hijo mío, que estás en los cielos,
Lleva a mis dos hijos este ramo de rosas de Francia y que todo el cielo
Se perfume por un año entero.

Un hurra se propaga
Como cien mil campanas.
Hurra lanzado de abismo en abismo
Entre nubes rocosas y la chispa
Que brota del contacto.
                                        Es el mismo,
El mismo corazón del aire intacto.
La eternidad sobre el naufragio
Y sobre ambos la confianza temblante del ala
Inclinada del uno al otro borde del vacío.
Es el mismo. Es la imagen del hombre que en el aire resbala,
Lleva sombras ajenas, olor de nuevos astros,
Y como un perro va siguiendo rastros
Por la Vía Láctea
        Es él.
                    Es el mismo,
Blanco sobre el abismo,
Señor y dueño
Del tiempo y del espacio.
Hermoso. Hermoso
En las marmolerías del sueño.

Men slept like a weary army
When the air felt your propeller's song and the weight of your winged
[motor –
Tamer of horizons and destinies,
Missionary on new roads
When people knew you were in the skies they awakened,
Millions of eyes raised in one prayer,
And the world came alive like a drum.

France, mother of aviation and of so many great things,
Welcomes you and applauds you more than anyone.
She who has just lost two sons in equal desire
Whispers in your ear:
"My son, who art in the heavens,
Bring my two sons this bouquet of roses from France and let all the sky
Be perfumed for one whole year."

A hurrah goes up
Like a hundred thousand bells.
Hurrah! thrown from abyss to abyss
Amongst clouds of stone and sparks
Firing from the contact.
It is the same,
The very heart of the air intact.
Eternity over the wreck
And over both the trembling confidence of a wing
Tilted from one edge of space to another.
It is the same. It is the image of a man gliding through the air,
Carrying remote shadows, the whiff of new worlds,
And like a dog following a scent
Along the Milky Way
It is he.
The very same,
White over the abyss
Lord and master
Of time and space.
Beautiful. Beautiful
In the marble works of dreams.

Tu cabeza en el cielo, el cielo es tu corona de estrellas silenciosas.
Una nube te trae un ramo de rosas
Y tú miras de arriba el pobre globo sembrado de cruces,
Este planeta nuestro que pasa en el vacío
Lento, lento y lleno de luces
Como un acorazado siguiendo la corriente de un río.

La vida. La tierra.
¿Ves? ¡Qué cosa absurda!
Un camello hace el ritmo del desierto,
Un tren que marcha,
Un hombre que piensa,
Una mujer que baila,
Un cementerio lejos como un rebaño muerto
Y un oso solo,
Lamiendo el eje de la tierra en medio del polo.

Hoy vuelves como un cometa con tu manto de victoria
Y una bandada de aplausos agita sus alas y vuela hacia tu gloria.
El cielo está bordado de tu nombre
Y como en un día de fiesta se ha llenado de encajes.
Niño imprudente, tenías poco más de veinte años de sonrisas
Y eras alegre como una isla después de un largo viaje.
Ahora tendrás que soportar la seriedad de cien millones de hombres.

Pero no importa, porque tu acto
Hace todo más puro, hace todo más alto,
Eleva las montañas, eleva las llanuras
(Las cordilleras tienen mil metros más),
Levanta el entusiasmo de las almas más duras.

Y por eso en mi lengua española,
En mi lengua que tiene balanceos de ola;
La lengua que se hablaba en las tres carabelas
Que encontraron la tierra donde viste la luz,
Te saludo y te canto. Me recuerda tu hazaña
La historia de mi raza, las proezas de España.

Your head in the sky, the sky is your crown of silent stars.
A cloud brings you a bouquet of roses
And from above you see the poor globe sewn with crosses,
This planet of ours that passes through the void
Slowly, slowly, and filled with lights
Like a warship drifting with the river current.

Life. The Earth.
            Do you see? How absurd it is!
A camel creates the rhythm of the desert,
A train speeding,
A man thinking,
A woman dancing,
A cemetery far away like a dead flock
And a lone bear,
Licking the axis of the earth at the centre of the Pole.

Now you return like a comet with your mantle of victory
And an echelon of applause flaps its wings and flies towards your glory.
The heavens are embroidered with your name
And are decked with lace, as on a feast day.
Imprudent child, you had little more than twenty years of smiles
And you were happy like an island after a long voyage.
Now you have to support the seriousness of a hundred million people.

But no matter, since your deed
Makes everything purer, elevates everything,
It raises the mountains, it raises the plains,
(The mountain ranges are a thousand metres higher),
It arouses enthusiasm in the hardest of souls.

And that is why, in my Spanish tongue,
In my language that has rolling waves,
The language spoken on the three caravels
That discovered the land where you saw the light,
I salute you and sing to you. Your deeds recall for me
The history of my race, the exploits of Spain.

POEMAS DE OCASIÓN

OCCASIONAL POEMS

PASIÓN, PASIÓN Y MUERTE

Señor, hoy es el aniversario de tu muerte.
Hace mil novecientos veintiséis años tú estabas en una cruz
Sobre una colina llena de gente.
Entre el cielo y la tierra tus ojos eran toda la luz.
Gota a gota sangraste sobre la historia.
Desde entonces un arroyo rojo atraviesa los siglos regando nuestra memoria.

Las horas se pararon ante el umbral extrahumano.
El tiempo quedó clavado con tus pies y tus manos.

Aquellos martillazos resuenan todavía,
Como si alguien llamara a las puertas de la vida.
Señor, perdóname si te hablo en un lenguaje profano.
Mas no podría hablarte de otro modo, pues soy esencialmente pagano.

Por si acaso eres Dios, vengo a pedirte una cosa
En olas rimadas con fatigas de prosa.

Hay en el mundo una mujer, acaso la más triste, sin duda la más bella
Protégela, Señor, sin vacilar; es ella.
Y si eres realmente Dios y puedes más que mi amor,
Ayúdame a cuidarla de todos los peligros, Señor.

Señor, te estoy mirando con los brazos abiertos.
Quisieras estrechar todos los hombres y todo el universo.

Señor, cuando doblaste tu cabeza sobre la eternidad
Las gentes no sabían si era de tus ojos que brotaba la oscuridad.

Las estrellas se fueron una a una en silencio
Y la luna no hallaba cómo esconderse detrás de los cerros.

PASSION, PASSION AND DEATH

Lord, today is the anniversary of Thy death.
One thousand nine hundred and twenty six years ago thou wert on a cross
On a hill filled with people.
Between the sky and the earth Thine eyes were all the light.
Drop by drop thou bledst into history.
Since then a red stream runs through the centuries irrigating our memory.

Time stopped at the superhuman threshold.
Time remained nailed with Thy feet and hands.

Those hammer blows still resound,
As if someone were knocking at the doors of life.
Lord, forgive me if I address Thee with profane language.
But I could not address Thee otherwise, for I am basically pagan.

Just in case Thou *art* God, I come to beg one thing of Thee
In waves rhymed with the weariness of prose.

In this world there is a woman, perhaps the saddest, without doubt
the most beautiful
Protect her, Lord, without hesitation; it is she.
And if Thou art truly God and canst do more than my love may do,
Help me to guard her from all danger, Lord.

Lord, I observe Thee with thine arms outstretched.
Thou wouldst wish to embrace all mankind and all the universe.

Lord, when Thou bowed'st Thine head over eternity
People knew not if it was from Thine eyes that the darkness appeared.

One by one the stars disappeared in silence
And the moon could not manage to hide behind the hills.

Se rasgaron las cortinas del cielo
Cuando pasaba tu alma al vuelo,
Y yo sé lo que se vio detrás; no fue una estrella,
Señor; fue la cara más bella.
La misma que verías al momento
Si rompieras la carne de mi pecho.

Como tú, Señor, tengo los brazos abiertos aguardándola a ella.
Así lo he prometido y me fatigan tantos siglos de espera.

Se me caen los brazos como aspas rotas sobre la tierra.
¿No podrías, Señor, adelantar la fecha?

Señor, en la noche de tu cielo ha pasado un aerolito
Llevándose un voto suyo y su mirada al fondo del infinito.
Hasta el fin de los siglos seguirá rodando nuestro anhelo allí escrito.

Señor, ahora de verdad estoy enfermo,
Una angustia insufrible me está mascando el pecho.
Y ese aerolito me señala el camino.
Amarró nuestras vidas en un solo destino.
Nos ha enlazado el alma mejor que todo anillo.

Señor, ella es débil y tenue como un ramo de sollozos.
Mirarla es un vértigo de estrellas en el fondo de un pozo.

Los ruiseñores del delirio cantaban en sus besos.
Se llenaba de fiebre el tubo de los huesos.

Alguien plantó en su alma viles hierbas de duda y ya no cree en mí.
Pruébame que eres Dios y en tres días de plazo llévame de aquí.

Quiero evadirme de mí mismo.
Mi espíritu está ciego y rueda entre planetas llenos de cataclismos.

Mi vida también sangra sobre la nieve,
Como un lobo herido que hace temblar la noche cada vez que se mueve.

The curtains of heaven were torn
As Thy soul flew past,
And I know what could be seen behind them; it was no star.
Lord; it was the most beautiful face.
The very same that Thou wouldst see now
If Thou wouldst pierce the flesh of my breast.

Like Thee, Lord, I have my arms outstretched, awaiting her.
This promise have I made and I am wearied by so many centuries waiting.

My arms fall like broken blades upon the earth.
Couldst Thou, Lord, not bring forward the date?

Lord, a shooting star has crossed Thy night sky
Bearing its vow and its gaze to the very depths of infinity.
Our longing inscribed there will roll ever onward until the end of time.

Lord now I am really sick,
An unbearable anguish is gnawing at my breast.
And that shooting star shows me the way.
It tied our lives into one single destiny.
Our souls are now bound together better than by any ring.

Lord, she is fragile and slender as a bouquet of sobs.
To look at her is vertigo of stars at the bottom of a well.

Nightingales of delirium sang in her kisses.
Her bone marrow burned with fever.

Someone planted foul weeds of doubt in her soul and now she no longer
believes in me.
Prove to me Thou art God and within three days take me away from here.

I want to escape from my self.
My spirit is blind and reels past planets full of cataclysms.

My life too bleeds onto the snow,
Like a wounded wolf that makes the night tremble with its every move.

Estoy crucificado sobre todas las cimas.
Me clava el corazón una corona de espinas.

Las lanzas de sus ojos me hieren el costado
Y un reguero de sangre sobre el silencio te dirá que he pasado.

Hace unos cuantos meses, Señor, abandoné mi viejo París,
Un extraño destino me trajo a sufrir en mi país.

Hace frío, hace frío. El viento empuja el frío sobre nuestros caminos
Y los astros enrollan la noche girando como molinos.

Señor, piensa en los pobres inmigrantes que vienen hacia América de oro
Y encuentran un sepulcro en vez de cajas de tesoros.

Ellos impregnan las olas del ritmo de sus cantares,
La tempestad de sus almas es más horrenda que la de todos los mares.

Míralos cómo lloran por los seres que no verán más;
Les gritan en la noche todas las cosas que dejaron atrás.

Señor, piensa en las pobrecitas que sufren al humillar su carne,
Las nuevas Magdalenas que hoy lloran el dolor de tu madre.

Agazapadas al fondo de la angustia de su absurda Babel,
Beben lentamente grandes vasos de hiel.

Señor, piensa en las espirales de los naufragios anónimos,
En los sueños truncados que estallan en pedazos de bólido.

Piensa en los ciegos que tienen los párpados llenos de música y lloran
        por los ojos de su violín.
Ellos frotan sus arcos sobre la vida en una amargura sin fin.

Señor, te he visto sangrando en los vitraux de Chartres,
Como mil mariposas que hacia los sueños parten.

I am crucified on all the summits.
A crown of thorns pierces my heart.

The lances of her eyes wound my side
And a trail of blood across the silence will tell Thee what has happened.

A few months ago, Lord, I abandoned my old Paris,
A strange fate brought me to suffer in my native land.

It is cold, it is cold. The wind drives the cold over our paths
And stars turning like mill-wheels roll up the night.

Lord, think of the poor immigrants who come to golden America
And find a tomb instead of treasure chests.

They impregnate the waves with the rhythm of their songs,
The storm of their souls is more horrifying than that of all the seas.

Look at them weeping for those they will see no more;
They cry out to them at night of all the things they left behind.

Lord, think of the poor women who suffer the humiliation of the flesh,
New Magdalens who today weep with Thy mother's pain.

Huddled in the depths of their absurd Babel of anguish,
They slowly drink large glasses of gall.

Lord, think of the spirals of anonymous shipwrecks,
Of the broken dreams that explode into pieces like meteors.

Think of the blind men whose eyelids are full of music and who weep
    through the eyes of their violins.
They scrape their bows over life in endless bitterness.

Lord, I have seen Thee bleeding in the stained-glass at Chartres,
Like a thousand butterflies vanishing into dreams.

Señor, en Venecia he visto tu rostro bizantino
Un día en que el aire se rompía de besos y de vino.

Las góndolas pasaban cantando como nidos,
Entre las ramas de olas, siguiendo nuestras risas hacia el Lido.

Y tú quedabas solo en San Marcos, aspirando las selvas de oraciones
Que crecen a tus plantas en todas las estaciones.

Señor, te he visto en un icono, obra de un monje serbio que al pintar
tus espinas
Sentía toda el alma llena de golondrinas.

En la historia del mundo, ¿qué significas tú?
Hace año y medio discutí este tema en un café de Moscú.

Un sabio ruso no te daba mayor importancia.
Yo decía haber creído en ti en mi infancia.

Una bailarina célebre por su belleza
Decía que tú eres solamente un cuento de tristeza.

Todos te negaron y ningún gallo cantó:
Acaso Pedro oyéndonos lloró.

Y al fondo de una vieja Biblia tu sermón de la montaña
Seguía resonando de una manera extraña.

Señor, yo también tengo mi vía dolorosa, mis caídas y mi pasión;
Saltando meridianos como un tigre herido, sangra y aúlla mi corazón.

Reina el amor en todas sus espléndidas catástrofes internas,
Mil rubíes al fondo del cerebro atruenan,
Y las plantas del deseo bordan el aire de estas noches eternas.

Poeta, poeta esclavo de aventuras y de algún sortilegio,
Soporto como tú la vida, el mayor sacrilegio.

Lord, in Venice I have seen Thy Byzantine face
On a day when the air was bursting with kisses and wine.

Gondolas went by singing like nests
Amongst wave branches, following our laughter towards the Lido.

And Thou remain'dst alone in Saint Mark's, inhaling the forests of prayers
That make Thy plants grow through all the seasons.

Lord, I have seen Thee in an icon, the work of a Serbian monk who
        when painting thy thorns
Felt his entire soul fill with swallows.

In the history of the world, of what significance art Thou?
A year and a half ago I debated this subject in a Moscow café.

A Russian sage attached no significance to Thee.
I said I had believed in Thee as a child.

A ballerina celebrated for her beauty
Said Thou wert no more than a tale of sadness.

Everyone denied Thee and no cock crowed:
Perhaps Peter wept upon hearing us.

And at the back of an old Bible Thy sermon on the mount
Kept echoing in some strange fashion.

Lord, I too have my *via dolorosa*, my falls and my passion;
Jumping over meridians like an wounded tiger, my heart bleeds and howls.

Love reigns in all its splendid internal catastrophes,
A thousand rubies thunder deep in my mind,
And the plants of desire embroider the air of these everlasting nights.

Poet, poet enslaved by adventures and under some kind of spell,
Like Thee I endure life, the greatest sacrilege.

Señor, lo único que vale en la vida es la pasión.
Vivimos para uno que otro momento de exaltación.

Un precipicio de suspiros se abre a mis pies; me detengo y vacilo.
Luego como un sonámbulo atravieso el mundo en equilibrio.

Señor, qué te importa lo que digan los hombres.
Al fondo de la historia
Eres un crepúsculo clavado en un madero de dolor y de gloria.

Y el arroyo de sangre que brotó en tu costado
Todavía, Señor, no se ha estancado.

Lord, the only thing that matters in life is passion.
We live for a moment or two of exaltation.

A precipice of sighs opens at my feet; I hold back, I waver.
Then like a sleepwalker I traverse the world on a tightrope.

Lord, what does it matter to Thee what men say.
In the depths of history
Thou art a twilight nailed to a wooden cross of pain and glory.

And the stream of blood that flows from Thy side,
Lord, has still not been staunched.

ELEGÍA A LA MUERTE DE LENIN

Más que el canto de la vid
Más que la muerte misma
Más que el dolor del recuerdo
Más que la angustia del tiempo
Es tu presencia en el alma del mundo

Tu nombre de alto clima
Tu corazón de fuegos dominados
Al entrar en la tumba
Fuiste como un sol de repente en el invierno
Fuiste como un verano en la muerte
Contigo la muerte se hace más grande que la vida

Los siglos reculan ante tu tumba
Selvas y ríos vienen en peregrinación
Y los países se arrodillan
Las ciudades desfilan como banderas y como quioscos de música
Las aldeas más lejanas son coronas ardientes

El sol distribuye flores en los caminos para tu fiesta
Que es la fiesta del hombre
Las olas saltan unas sobre otras para llegar primero
A traerte el saludo de sus comarcas remotas
El ruido de los mares
Se confunde con el canto de las multitudes
Tu muerte crea un nuevo aniversario

Más grande que el aniversario de una montaña
Has vencido has vencido
Una fecha tan profunda corno ésta no han labrado los hombres
Has abierto las puertas de la nueva era
Tu estatura se levanta corno un cañonazo que parte en dos la historia
[humana

ELEGY ON THE DEATH OF LENIN

Greater than the song from the vine
Greater than death itself
Greater than the pain of memory
Greater than the anguish of time
Is your presence in the soul of the world

Your name lofty as the climate
Your heart of tempered flames
Upon entering the tomb
You were like sudden sunshine in Winter
You were like a Summer within death
With you death becomes greater than life

The centuries recoil before your grave
Forests and rivers come in pilgrimage
And nations kneel
Cities parade like banners and like bandstands
The farthest villages are burning wreaths

The sun scatters flowers along the roads for your festival
Which is the festival of mankind
Waves leap over one other to get there first
To bring you greetings from their remote districts
The roar of the seas
Mingles with the singing of crowds
Your death creates a new anniversary

Greater than the jubilee of a mountain
You have triumphed you have triumphed
No date as profound as this has ever been carved out by human hand
You opened the gates to a new era
Your stature increases like a cannon shot splitting human history in two.

Un hombre ha pasado por la tierra
Y ha dejado cálida la tierra para muchos siglos

Contigo la muerte se hace más grande que la vida

Tú eres la nobleza del hombre
En ti empieza un nuevo linaje universal

Y así como tu vida era la vid de la vida
Tu muerte será la muerte de la muerte

Un hombre ha derrumbado las montañas
Al fondo de los siglos se oyen los pasos de millones de esclavos
Se van alejando sobre el tiempo y el tiempo retumba de eco en eco

No hay más distancia de una tribu a otra
Tu voz de semilla que traen los vientos venerables
Tu voz Lenin cambia la raza humana
Y hace una sola tierra de tantas tierras hostiles
Tú eres la forma de los siglos que vienen
Tú eres el sosias del futuro
El bramido del odio vuelto canto de amor
Obedeciendo a los impulsos de la tierra
Gritaste a las conciencias que no sentían el gran ritmo
Tu clarín no permite que haya disidentes
Sombras que se caen del hombre y se dejan morir sobre las rutas

Un hombre ha pasado por la tierra
Y ha dejado su corazón ardiendo entre los hombres
Tú eres la imagen de los siglos que vienen
Y ésa es la voz del sembrador

Los hombres levantan sus martillos
Los martillos se quedan suspensos en el aire
Levantan sus hoces y las hoces se quedan en la luz
Todos oyen todos oímos

A man has walked the earth
And has left the earth warm for centuries to come

With you death becomes greater than life

You are the nobility of humanity
In you there begins a new universal lineage

And thus as your life was the vine of life
Your death will be the death of death

A man has toppled mountains
At the end of time, the footsteps of millions of slaves can be heard
Fading away through time and time reverberates from echo to echo

No longer is there distance between one tribe and another
Your voice a seed carried by venerable winds
Your voice Lenin transforms the human race
Making one earth out of so many hostile lands
You are the shape of centuries to come
You are the future's doppelgänger
The roar of hatred turned into a song of love
Obeying the impulses of the earth
You cried out to consciences that had no feel for the great rhythm
Your clarion allows for no dissidents
No shadows falling away from humanity and left to die on the roads

A man has walked the earth
And he has left his heart burning amongst humanity
You are the image of centuries to come
Yours is the voice of the sower

Men raise their hammers
The hammers remain suspended in the air
They raise their sickles and the sickles stay glowing in the light
They all hear we all hear

Ese latir de tu corazón más allá de la muerte
Ese latir de tu corazón que te vuelve a nosotros y te hace presente

Podrías decir desde la muerte
Estrellas yo puse en marcha a los hombres

Eres el ruido de una aurora que se levanta
Eres el ruido de todo un mundo que trabaja de todo un mundo que canta
Eres el ruido de un astro victorioso recorriendo el espacio

Qué lenguaje es ése que golpea las rocas de la orilla
Qué aliento es ése que ondea los trigales infinitos
Qué palabras son ésas que iluminan la noche
Y ese latir de tu corazón más allá de la muerte
Hemos recogido tus palabras
Para que todo sea humano y verdadero
Para hacer hombre al hombre
Y cuando tu voz haya resonado en todo el mundo
Los tristes los siervos los ilotas
Desaparecerán en las profundas madrigueras
Y saldrán hombres por todos los caminos
Qué lenguaje es ése que mata el hambre y apaga la sed
Qué palabras son ésas que visten de calor
Saltan las cadenas y con ellas salta el hombre

Y se oye ese latir de tu corazón más allá de la muerte

El hombre que hace gemir el yunque
El hombre que hace llorar la piedra
El hombre que lanza las semillas cerradas a los surcos
El hombre que levanta casas
El hombre que construye puentes
Y el que escucha el canto de los pájaros
Y el que cuenta las estrellas sentado en medio de la noche
El hombre que fabrica instrumentos y máquinas
El hombre que cambia la manera de las cosas
Y las formas de la tierra

That beating of your heart from beyond death
That beating of your heart that returns you to us and makes you present

You could say from beyond death
Stars I set humanity in motion

You are the sound of a rising dawn
You are the sound of a whole world at work a whole world singing
You are the sound of a victorious star streaking through space

What language is that which strikes the rocks on the shore
What breath is that which rustles the infinite wheat fields
What words are those that light up the night
And that beating of your heart beyond death
We have gathered your words
So that all may be human and true
To make humanity human
And once your voice has resonated throughout the world
Those who are sad the servants the helots
Will vanish into their deep burrows
And men will emerge on every road
What language is this that kills hunger and quenches thirst
What words are those that clothe us with warmth
Break the chains and with them the man breaks free

And we can hear your heart beating beyond death

The man who makes anvils groan
The man who makes stones weep
The man who throws closed seeds into furrows
The man who raises houses
The man who builds bridges
And the one who listens to birdsong
And the one who counts the stars sitting in the middle of the night
The man who makes tools and machines
The man who changes the shape of things
And the forms of the earth

El hombre que amasa el pan y tiene olor a levadura en la mirada
El hombre que conduce rebaños de montaña en montaña
El hombre que guía caravanas en los desiertos más largos que su
        propia memoria

Todos oyen
Ese latir de tu corazón más allá de la muerte
Tu corazón repicando adentro del sepulcro

Contigo la muerte se hace más grande que la vida
Los siglos reculan ante tu tumba
Selvas y ríos vienen en peregrinación
Y los países se arrodillan

Desde hoy nuestro deber es defenderte de ser dios

The man who kneads bread and has the scent of yeast in his eyes
The man who drives flocks from mountain to mountain
The man who has led caravans across deserts for longer than he can
remember

All of them can hear
That beating of your heart beyond death
Your heart tolling inside the grave

With you death becomes greater than life
The centuries recoil before your tomb
Forests and rivers come in pilgrimage
And nations kneel

From this day forward our duty is to defend you from becoming a god

DESPERTAR DE OCTUBRE 1917

Redoblan los tambores de la sangre
Y el dolor de los tiempos se levanta con los puños erguidos
Toca a diana el clarín de los siglos
Sobre las tierras y los mares
Despertad proletarios sacudid las melenas de león
Como el ramaje iracundo de las olas
O como esa bandera que palpita en el cielo
Esa bandera color de corazón

Un mundo se derrumba y otro se yergue
Una procesión camina lenta hacia la muerte
Y otra marcha cantando hacia la vida
Una es el pasado que se esconde
La otra es el mañana que se despierta y que vibra
Como el ala del día

Los planetas renacen los ríos se detienen
Cambio toda mi vida por esa estrella nueva
Las flores dicen versos las colinas escuchan
Cambio por vuestros puños los gritos de mi boca
Cambio vuestro sudor por mis palomas

Volved a las grutas funerarias
Enemigos del hombre y su destino
No queremos ver vuestros rostros de yeso
Ni oír vuestros pasos de lobo en el camino

Fantasma del pasado yo no fui tu pastor
Yo no aplaudí tus días ni conté tus diamantes
Y o no nutrí tus pájaros ni agrandé tus montañas
Cuida tus cabellos debajo de la tierra
Cuida tu carne que gusta a las raíces
Serás útil al fin en el silencio de la tumba

THE AWAKENING OF OCTOBER 1917

The drums of blood roll
And the pain of the times rises with raised fists
The bugle of the centuries sounds reveille
Over land and sea
Wake up proletarians shake your leonine manes
Like the angry branches of waves
Or like that flag fluttering in the sky
That heart-coloured flag

One world crumbles and another rises
A procession moves slowly towards death
And another marches singing towards life
One is the past hiding itself away
The other is the future waking and vibrating
Like the wings of dawn.

Planets are reborn rivers pause
I would trade my whole life for that new star
The flowers recite verses the hills listen
I will trade your fists the screams from my mouth
I will trade your sweat for my doves

Return to your funerary caverns
Enemies of humanity and its destiny
We do not wish us to see your plaster faces
Nor hear your wolf-like tread on the path

Phantom from the past I was not your shepherd
I did not applaud your days nor count your diamonds
And I did not feed your birds nor make your mountains bigger
Tend to your hair beneath the earth
Tend to your flesh, savoured by the roots
At last you will be useful in the silence of the tomb

Tu sangre será savia
Tus brazos serán ramas
Y tus dedos perdidos serán frutas

Hombre eres hombre y no lo sabías
Tuya es la tierra y el cielo que dominas
Tuya la inmensa curva de los mares
Como es tuyo tu esfuerzo
Y el humo de tus fábricas escaleras del aire
Y el trigo de tus surcos amado por el viento

Hombre eres hombre y no lo sabías
Pero hoy los clarines rojos te lo dicen
Te lo gritan los árboles
Te lo cantan los mares
Despierta de tu sueño ya no eres más esclavo
Eres hombre sal de ti mismo sal de tus profundidades muéstrate al sol
Liberta tus fuerzas despliega tus energías
Eres hombre eres hombre

Your blood will become sap
Your arms will become branches
And your lost fingers will become fruit

Human you are human and did not know it
Yours is the earth and the sky that you command
Yours is the vast curve of the seas
As your efforts are yours
And the smoke of your factories stairways to the air
And the wheat in your furrows beloved by the wind

Human you are human and did not know it
But today the red bugles proclaim it to you
The trees shout it to you
The seas sing it to you
Awake from your slumber you are a slave no longer
You are human leave yourself behind come out of your depths show
yourself to the sun
Unleash your strength unleash your energies
You are human you are human

CANTO AL PRIMERO DE MAYO

Hoy el mundo florece en nuestros ojos
el Primero de Mayo es el tambor
que despierta a la tropa proletaria
como la selva cuando llama el sol.

Hoy todos los obreros de la tierra
vibramos como un solo corazón.

Y a pronto lavará nuestra miseria
el Alba de la Gran Revolución
saltarán al espacio las cadenas
y temblará el burgués explotador.

Hoy todos los obreros de la tierra
vibramos como un solo corazón.

Hoy nuestras almas son banderas rojas
el Primero de Mayo es un tambor
Y galopa en el aire como el trueno
cuando las nubes lloran de terror.

Hoy todos los obreros de la tierra
vibramos como un solo corazón.

El Primero de Mayo nos recuerda
día de gloria y días de dolor
es la fiesta del mundo proletario
es el día de luto del patrón.

Hoy todos los obreros de la tierra
vibramos como un solo corazón.

SONG FOR MAY DAY

Today the world blossoms in our eyes
May Day is the drum
that awakens the proletarian ranks
like the jungle when summoned by the sun.

Today all we workers on earth
vibrate as one heart.

And soon our misery will be washed away
by the Dawn of the Great Revolution
chains will be shatter in the air
and the exploiting bourgeois will tremble.

Today all we workers on earth
vibrate as one heart.

Today our souls are red flags
May Day is a drum
galloping through the air like thunder
while the clouds weep in terror.

Today all we workers on earth
vibrate as one heart.

May Day reminds us
days of glory and days of sorrow
it is the festival of the proletarian world
it is the patron saint's day of mourning.

Today all we workers on earth
vibrate as one heart.

Millones de almas en un mismo ideal
formemos un solo hombre universal.
            Los puños levantad
            por la Internacional.

Millones de hombres cantan su canción
vibrando con un solo corazón.

Millions of souls with one ideal
let us form a single universal man.
        Raise your fists
        for the Internationale.

Millions of men sing their song
vibrating as a single heart.

URSS

De allí viene ese viento sordo a la muerte
Sin espectros sin sonido de cadenas respiradas
De allí viene el aire aplaudiendo delirante de pechos encendido por sus
rayos y sus truenos
De la URSS vienen las alas a nacer en las espaldas de todos los hombre
De la URSS viene la savia electrizada de esperanzas
Porque la URSS es el primer país que se da como una espiga
Que se da sin reservas entero generado en resplandores
Es el primer país en la historia de los tiempos en donde está naciendo
el hombre
En donde el hombre está dejando de ser bestia
En donde la humanidad sale de la emboscada
Y el cerebro respira
El cerebro se hace cimiento y simiente de soles conquistados
En la alianza de las mareas y las selvas nuevas
Para enterrar el tiempo agusanado y levantar los otros horizontes
Las montañas se desvelan contrarias a sus instintos
Se diría que el hombre antes no tuvo alma
La claridad se abre saludando a Lenin
Que pasa sobre el monumento de sus huellas
Con la Tierra que le sigue
Con los hombres presentidos como pequeñas lámparas
La Tierra que él dio a los hombres
Los hombres que él dio a la Tierra

Ya no queda ni el recuerdo vagabundo
Del padrecito Zar que no conoció la justicia hasta que una bala le
reventó los sesos
Y la Zarina con la mirada llena de perlas y los ojos tan inteligentes
como ostras
Y las misas cantadas entre pechos decorados con oros medallas obispos
ministros y generales con asma
He aquí el esqueleto del pasado el cadáver elegante la podredumbre
que sólo en el silencio de la ceniza puede lavar

USSR

There comes that wind deaf to death
No spectres no sound of dragging chains
There comes the air clapping deliriously with chestfuls of fire ignited by
    its thunder and lightning
From the USSR come wings born to sprout on the backs of all mankind
From the USSR comes the electrified sap of hope
Because the USSR is the first country to offer itself as a sheaf of wheat
To give of itself entirely unreservedly born in splendour
It is the first country in the history of time where man is being born
Where man ceases to be a beast
Where humanity emerges from ambush
And the mind can breathe
The mind becomes foundation and seed of conquered suns
In alliance with the tides and new forests
Burying the worm-eaten past to raise different horizons
Mountains are watchful defying their instincts
It would seem man never had a soul
Clarity breaks opens with a salute to Lenin
Who strides over the monument of his legacy
With the Earth following him
With men foreseen like little lamps
The Earth he gave to mankind
The men he gave to the Earth

Not even a wandering memory remains
Of the Tsar the little father who knew no justice until a bullet blew his
    brains out
Or the Tsarina with her gaze full of pearls and eyes as intelligent as oysters
Or the masses sung amongst chests adorned with gold medals bishops
    ministers and asthmatic generals
Here lies the skeleton of the past the elegant corpse the rot that can only
    be cleansed by the silence of ash

Pero he aquí que la URSS hizo el aire respirable lavó la atmósfera a
grandes chorros
La URSS es el gran río donde muere la noche
Y empieza la divisoria luz sobre su tallo dominante
Sus cimientos explosivos espantan a los pechos cubiertos de sepulcros
Que no ven la razón del estruendo ni el comienzo de otro campo
La URSS arrastra un sedimento de vida y de músicas nacientes
Ella coloca la primera piedra del alma humana
En esa tierra de sueños alcanzados por las manos
Se amasa el pan del más alto destino
Imperioso lo mismo que la infancia o que el sol al empezar su día
Allí se labran los caminos
Esos caminos puros como la marcha virgen
Ídolos de aliento
Y la vejez de las raíces con su sal con su llanto y sus tinieblas esperando
el yunque de los futuros relámpagos
Allí se multiplican las escuelas
Y es la alegría del alma con los nudos desatados
Es la miel resucitando el cementerio

Allí crecen las bibliotecas incansables como selvas con sus frutos de miradas
infinitas
La URSS inmensa fiebre y colmena de mares que ofrecen su sangre
La URSS en los brazos de millones de entusiasmos subiendo sin vértigos
subiendo

Gloria del hombre necesario a las estrellas
Y en el silencio amoblado de años y de admiración
Se agiganta el andar de los creadores unidos a la luz
Pasos de un pueblo de deseos gritos manchados de llamas
Y esas espadas en la tumba y esas torres cayendo en ruinas sobre su leyenda

Allí los ríos navegables dando su lirio intacto
Allí los campos de recreo para las manos de acero fatigado para los
ojos que cambian primavera por primavera
Los humos de todas las usinas abrazándose en el cielo sin patria cual
su luna y el amor

But behold, the USSR has made the air breathable and cleansed the
atmosphere with great torrents
The USSR is the great river where night dies
And the dividing light begins to shine on its dominant stem
Its explosive foundations terrify hearts already entombed
Which see neither the reason for the clamour nor the start of a new field
The USSR carries with it a sediment of life and nascent music
It lays the foundation stone of the human soul
In that soil of dreams reached by hands
Here the bread of highest destiny is kneaded
As irresistible as childhood or the sun at daybreak
Here roads are being carved out
Those roads unsullied like the virgin's procession
Idols of encouragement
And the ancient roots with their salt with their weeping and their shadows
awaiting the anvil of future lightning bolts
Here schools are multiply
And the soul rejoices with its knots untied
It is honey resurrecting the cemetery

Here libraries grow tirelessly like forests bearing fruits of infinite gazes
The USSR immense fever and hive of oceans offering their lifeblood
The USSR borne on the arms of millions of fervent hearts rising with no
vertigo rising

Glory to mankind needed by the stars
And in the silence furnished with years and admiration
The pacing of creators united by the light increases dramatically
Footsteps of a people filled with desire cries streaked with flames
And those swords in the tomb and those towers falling in ruins over their
own legend

There navigable rivers offering their lilies intact
There fields are playgrounds for hands of weary steel for eyes that change
Spring after Spring
The smoke from all the factories embracing in a sky that has no homeland
just like its moon and its love

El cielo que labra la tierra y canta la Internacional como un rubí de
atardecer
Los nuevos templos donde se fabrica el agrado de la vida y la facilidad
de nuestras horas
Allí se cuajan los inventos se gestan otras formas y otra esencia
Allí se ausculta el planeta con sus semillas y su nuevo sentido del vivir
Con sus posibilidades de inteligencia en flores contagiosas
Con esos grandes bolcheviques como estatuas del tiempo atravesando
el cielo como campanadas
Y se siembra un planeta distinto que no dice papá y mamá
Un planeta sin curas sin amos sin leyes hipócritas
Sin esos políticos que ganan el campeonato de natación en la baba de
sus propios discursos
Sin banqueros sin vampiros sin perros policiales y policiales perros
Sin alcancías sin milagros
Sin palmas agonizantes adentro de cada lágrima milenaria y desnuda
Porque allí las lágrimas tienen un arco-iris que las desborda

The sky that tills the earth and sings the Internationale like a ruby sunset
New temples where the pleasures of life and the ease of our hours is
manufactured
There inventions grow other forms and other essences
There the planet is examined with its seeds and its new sense of life
Its possibilities of intelligence in contagious flowers
With those great Bolsheviks like statues in time piercing the sky like
tolling bells
And a different planet is being sown that no longer says Papa or Mama
A planet with no priests no masters no hypocritical laws
With none of those politicians who are champions at swimming in the
slime of their own speeches
No bankers no vampires no police dogs and no dog-like police
No piggy banks no miracles
No dying palms inside each age-old naked tear
Because over there tears come from overflowing rainbows

LA DULZURA DE VIVIR

Tenéis hambre, tenéis frío
El banquero ríe a carcajadas
Con su risa de ángulo de acero.

Los vuestros mueren de miseria
El patrón ríe a carcajadas
Con su risa de fusta saliendo de la muerte.

Vuestros hijos en harapos viven como cerdos
El amo ríe a carcajadas
Y su risa ata la luz en las estrellas.

Estáis tristes, estáis desesperados
El gobernante ríe a carcajadas
Entre siglos perdidos y tinieblas hechas de larvas adecuada

Queréis educación, queréis justicia
El cura ríe a carcajadas
Como sepulcro desangrado bajo el oscuro extremo.

Vuestra vida rota grita venganza
El general ríe a carcajadas
Con su risa de lanza en el costado de la tierra.

Ríen porque saben que vosotros
Ignoráis vuestras fuerzas como la montaña que puede ser volcán.

Porque piensan que ellos con sus lacayos
Con sus curas de lengua subterránea y dulzona
Con sus gendarmes orgullosos de ser perros de guardia

THE SWEETNESS OF LIVING

You are hungry, you are cold
The banker roars with laughter
With a laugh sharp as steel edge.

Your loved ones are dying of misery
The landlord roars with laughter
His whip-like laugh drawn from death itself.

Your ragged children live like pigs
The boss roars with laughter
And his laughter tethers the light in the stars.

You are sad, you are desperate
The ruler roars with laughter
Amid centuries lost and darkness teeming with larvae

You wish for education, you wish for justice
The priest roars with laughter
Like a blood-soaked tomb beneath the dark end.

Your broken lives cry out for vengeance
The general roars with laughter
His laugh like a lance in the earth's side.

They laugh because they know you are all
Unaware of your strength like the mountain unaware it could be a volcano.

Because they think that with their lackeys
With their honeyed subterranean tongues
With their gendarmes proud of being watchdogs

Con sus señoras caritativas como flores de tumba
Con sus palabras untuosas elogiando la mansedumbre
No os dejarán salir del sueño de cisterna venenosa

Obreros del mundo daos la mano
Como lámpara y lámpara encontradas y unidas de repente

Mirad ese cuchillo bolchevique entre los labios
Del gran afiche para espantar palomas en la cuna
Ese cuchillo habituado a los dientes
Tan fácil a cortar risas de bestias sin conciencia
Carcajadas de muerte en olas de ceniza.

With their charitable ladies like flowers on a tomb
With their unctuous words praising meekness
They will not let you out of the poisoned reservoir of your dreams

Workers of the world clasp hands
Like lanterns suddenly found and brought together

Look at that Bolshevik knife between the lips
On that big poster for scaring doves in their cradles
That knife accustomed to teeth
So deft at cutting through the laughter of beasts with no conscience
Death's burst of laughter in waves of ash.

POLICÍAS Y SOLDADOS

El pobre policía como autómata ciego
Dando palos al Hombre de raíz planetaria
Mandobles al destino irremediable
Disparando sus armas contra el alba
Contra la luz que se despierta en un inmenso grito
Contra sus propios hermanos de pasado y futuro
Contra el obrero de su casta de su propia familia
Por defender a su enemigo
Por defender al que le paga como se paga a un esclavo
El que le compra su vida y su destino humano
Por algunas monedas sangrientas
Por algunas piltrafas de deshonra
Sin saberlo se asesina a sí mismo
En nombre de su amo y de su Dios Capitalismo

Y ese pobre soldado
Hijo de obrero y que fue obrero
Y que mañana volverá a ser obrero
Hoy asesina obreros
Asesina a sus hermanos
Asesina a sus compañeros
A los amigos de su padre a sus iguales
A los desheredados como él
Asesina inconsciente su propio porvenir
Y el porvenir del mundo
Asesina a la aurora de una mayor justicia
Asesina el ideal de un orden nuevo

Y esto en nombre de su enemigo
Del que le arroja el salario como bocado a un perro
Se asesina a sí mismo
En nombre del Dios Capitalismo

POLICEMEN AND SOLDIERS

The poor policeman like a blind automaton
Giving a beating to mankind rooted in the planet
Giving a blow to inescapable destiny
Firing his weapons at the dawn
At the light that awakens with a great cry
At his own past and future brethren
At the worker from his own class from his own family
For defending his enemy
For defending the one who pays him a slave's wages
The one who buys his life and his human destiny from him
For a few bloodstained coins
For some scraps of dishonour
Without realising it he kills himself
In the name of his master and his God Capitalism

And that poor soldier
Son of a worker who once was a worker
And who tomorrow will again be a worker
Today he kills workers
Kills his brothers
Kills his comrades
His father's friends his peers
The disinherited just like him
Unwittingly he kills his own future
And the future of the world
Kills the dawn of a greater justice
Kills the ideal of a new order

And this in the name of his enemy
The one who tosses him his wages like scraps to a dog
He kills himself
In the name of that God Capitalism

Pobres mastines inconscientes
Esperando la sonrisa del amo
Pobres fantoches engañados
Al volver a sus casas les espera
La hija de un obrero
La hermana de un obrero
Y ellos serán padres de obreros
Y acaso otros autómatas tan ciegos como ellos
Matarán a sus hijos porque sus hijos despertaron
Y no quisieron ser esclavos

Pobre soldado pobre guardián de su enemigo
Con tus manos teñidas de sangre proletaria
Acaricias a tu mujer y no piensas
Que ella es también sangre de obreros
Que ella es la sangre de tus víctimas
La misma sangre que asesinas

Pobre fantoche sin conciencia
Te pavoneas orgulloso en las calles que no son tuyas
Porque vistes casaca y llevas botones relucientes
Y olvidas que tu carne debajo de la farsa
Forma el cuerpo de un paria
Es la carne de un proletario
La carne despreciada por el amo
Que te manda a la muerte
Para aplastar a tus hermanos
Que te hace asesino
Para dormir tranquilo

Piensa que a cada obrero que asesinas
Pobre gendarme ciego te suicidas
Y tu conciencia
¿Cómo es que no despierta en tantos años?
Pobre soldado
¿Dónde está tu conciencia?
En el bolsillo de tu amo

Poor unwitting watchdogs
Waiting for the master's smile
Poor deluded puppets
When they return home there waiting for them are
A worker's daughter
A worker's sister
And they will be parents of workers
And perhaps other automata as blind as they
Will kill their children because their children have awoken
And no longer wanted to be slaves

Poor soldier poor guardian of his enemy
With your hands stained with proletarian blood
You caress your wife and do not think
That she too has the blood of workers
That she has the blood of your victims
The same blood that you kill

Poor puppet with no conscience
You strut proudly through streets that are not yours
Because you wear a uniform and shiny buttons
And you forget that your flesh beneath the display
Is the body of a pariah
The flesh of a proletarian
The flesh despised by the master
Who sends you to your death
To crush your brothers
Who makes you a killer
For a peaceful night's sleep

Think of every worker you kill
Poor blind gendarme you are killing yourself
And your conscience
How come it hasn't awoken after all these years?
Poor soldier
Where is your conscience?
In your master's pocket

ESTÁ SANGRANDO ESPAÑA

España, España. ¿Quién te ha llamado en las tinieblas?
Montaña de montañas ¿por qué lloras esta noche?
Sabes que tantos de tus hijos han muerto y tantos van a morir.
Pero esa muerte tiene por razón la Vida
Es el cimiento de sal que une las flores y los ríos y los mares
Esa muerte camina del ocaso hacia el alba
Ellos quieren vivir como hombres a cielo propio
Ellos son hijos de la tierra que se calienta entre sus manos
Ellos son hijos de la luz que se alegra con sus ojos.
No son bestias de tinieblas
No son estiércol
Ni están hechos para el hambre y para todo dolor,
Hombres como los hombres
Con una alegría de ser hermanos y de querer y de crear.

Oh máquina de recios fuegos. ¿Por qué lloras esta noche?
¿Por qué agoniza el viento como un pueblo de manos condenadas?
Y sería tan fácil tan fácil como luz repartida.

Un poco de cielo para la tierra
Un poco de tierra para el cielo
Y un arco-iris como un gran pájaro de enseñanzas
Para los hombres que todavía no comprenden
Para aquellos que aún no adivinan el sentido de este andar
Oh montaña ¿por qué te reclinas contra la noche?
¿Por qué lloras en su pecho?
Oh abuela de los ríos que crecen como flores a su destino
¿Por qué alzas tu voz terrible como un lamento de volcanes decididos?
Tempestad obligada a salir de sus tibios ramajes
Carne hecha clamor de edades dolorosas y aguardando su día.

Hay un olor a sangre entre las piedras.

SPAIN IS BLEEDING

Spain, Spain, who was it that called to you in the darkness?
Mountain of mountains why do you weep tonight?
You know so many of your children have died and that many more will die.
But Life is the reason for those deaths
It is the salt base binding flowers rivers and seas
That is Death walking from dusk to dawn
They want to live like men beneath their own sky
They are children of the earth that warms in their hands
They are children of the light that rejoices with their eyes.
They are not beasts of darkness
They are not filth
Nor are they made for hunger and all that pain,
Men like other men
With the joy of brotherhood of love and of creation.

O engine of fierce fires, why do you weep tonight?
Why does the wind suffer like a people with condemned hands?
And it would be as simple just as simple as light shared.

A little sky for the earth
A little earth for the sky
And a rainbow like a great teaching bird
For men who still do not understand
For those who have not yet guessed the meaning of this journey
Oh mountain why do you lean against the night?
Why do you weep on its breast?
O grandmother of rivers that grow like flowers towards their destiny
Why do you raise your terrible voice like the lament of resolute volcanoes?
A storm forced out of its warm branches
Flesh turned into an outcry of painful ages awaiting their day.

There is a smell of blood amongst the stones.

España se levanta como heroico mar con sus estrellas despertadas
Pueblos de hondos siglos con costumbres de sol y peñascos cantores
Que no quiere cadenas ni retornar al yugo
Pueblo hecho de dolor como en ritmo de rayos
Y tan dispuesto a ser libre, tan dispuesto a una alta vida
Que no le asusta la muerte.
Hay un olor a sangre en las raíces
Y hay un himno de luz que estremece al planeta
Como un gran porvenir anunciado de golpe entre las sombras.
He aquí la historia de la sangre
Unos hombres son duros, son insolentes y feroces
Otros hombres son sufrientes, son oprimidos e inconformes
Unos son victimarios y otros son víctimas
Hay unos que lo poseen todo como adherido a sus carnes y a sus huesos
Y otros que no poseen ni su sombra ni su esfuerzo en el brillo de la tierra
El hombre dueño de la existencia
El que se cree dueño de la vida
Porque se la ha robado y le ha puesto su sello de piedra venenosa
El que aplasta la vida como un animal muerto
El sembrador del odio, el insaciable de ojos corrosivos
No permite cabezas erguidas ni manos desatadas
No acepta otro destino al sol de su destino
No tolera el trabajo de todos para todos
Detesta la bondad y el derecho de ser hombre entre los hombres
Ama su goce pero le irrita el goce ajeno
Entonces los que no aceptan la injusticia
Yerguen los puños como rocas desesperadas en el fondo
Y hay un olor a sangre entre las hierbas
Y hay una gran promesa tras el llanto que se ilumina por sí solo

Ellos cambiaron el mundo
Los que no están contentos con el mundo
Hombres aplastados, hombres de vientre seco y pecho en horno de amargura
Hombres engañados y resueltos como selva invasora
Hombres llenos de un solo alarido
Hombres que cubren la tierra de los hombres

Spain rises like a heroic sea with its awakened stars
Centuries-old villages with sun-drenched customs and singing crags
Who do not want chains nor a return to the yoke
A people forged by pain in rhythms of lightning
And so willing to be free, so willing to live a noble life
That death does not frighten them.
There is a smell of blood in the roots
And there is a hymn of light shaking the planet
Like a great future suddenly revealed amidst the shadows.
Here is the history of blood
Some men are hard, they are insolent and fierce
Other men suffer, are oppressed and discontent.
Some are victimisers and others are victims
There are some who have it all as if it were attached to their flesh and bones
And others who own neither their shadow nor the fruits of their labour in
 the earth's bright light
The man who owns existence
The one who believes he owns life
Because he has stolen it and branded it with his poisonous stone seal
He who crushes life like a dead animal
The sower of hatred, insatiable, with corrosive eyes
He allows no heads held high nor hands unbound
He accepts no destiny but that lit by the sun of his own destiny
He does not tolerate the work of all for all
He despises goodness and the right to be a man among men
He loves his own pleasure but is irritated by the pleasure of others
So those who do not accept injustice
Raise their fists like desperate rocks in the depths
And there is a smell of blood amongst the grasses
And there is a great promise shining behind the tears

They changed the world
Those who are not happy with the world
Men crushed, men with dry bellies and hearts forged in bitter fire
Men deceived yet resolute like an encroaching jungle
Men filled with a single outcry
Men who cover the land of men

El Doloroso sale de su silencio cruzado de azotes
Sale de la antigua tiniebla hacia el espacio de altos resplandores
Sale del sudor en cadenas mortales
Como un cometa de manto legendario que alumbra el universo
Para anunciar un nuevo tiempo
Y hay un olor a sangre sobre la tarde de lenguaje cansado

Hay un olor a sangre en las Asturias
Asesinan los amos de la tierra
Asesinan al hombre que no quiere el andrajo
Los insaciables asesinan la dignidad que se difunde
Como los ríos fervorosos en ansias de otras formas
Mátalos amo ellos no quieren ser esclavos
Muérdelos perro de sepulcro, ellos jamás aceptarán su suerte
Despedázalos, asesínalos, dueño y señor del mundo
Nunca podrás vencer el ansia de luz de los relámpagos
Y los héroes caen en ruido de ramajes altivos y lluvia bondadosa
Caen a la historia iluminando las edades
Que nuestra tierra camaradas sea dulce cuanto será orgullosa
Que os de un sueño de gloria nutrido de siglos y de suaves raíces
Cantante arena que se desliza en los oídos
Y a otro lado la epopeya galopando en sus caballos y sus ruidos de ruedas
Camaradas tenemos el deber de cantar
No sólo el mar tendrá su voz
Camaradas nosotros también sabemos bendecir vuestro heroísmo

Vosotros cambiaréis la vida
Porque no estáis contentos con la vida que os ha falsificado el insaciable.

Y sigue la historia de los hechos
Una gran dama se presenta ante el hijo de un héroe
—Pobre niño, ¿tienes hambre?
—Sí, tengo hambre.
—¿Quieres pan?
—No quiero vuestro pan. Prefiero mi hambre.
No quiero el pan de los asesinos de mi padre.
—Niño rebelde. Yo soy la caridad. Yo te perdono.

The Man of Suffering emerges from his silence scarred by lashes
He emerges from ancient darkness into the space of splendid light
He emerges from sweat in deadly chains
Like a comet with a legendary mantle lighting up the universe
To herald a new era
And there is a smell of blood in the weary-tongued evening

There is a smell of blood in Asturias
They kill the owners of the land
They kill the man who will not accept rags
The insatiable kill the dignity that spreads
Like passionate rivers yearning for new forms
Slaughter them master they will not be slaves
Bite them, tomb hound, they will never accept their fate
Tear them to pieces, kill them, lord and master of the world
You will never conquer the lightning bolt's craving for light
And heroes fall to the sound of proud branches and gentle rain
They fall into history illuminating the ages
Comrades may our land be as sweet as it is proud
May it grant you dreams of glory nourished by centuries and soft roots
Singing sands slipping into your ears
While elsewhere the epic gallops on horseback and on rumbling wheels
Comrades we have a duty to sing
The sea will not be the lone voice
Comrades we too know how to bless your heroism

You will change life
Because you are not content with a life falsified by the insatiable.

And so the story goes on
A great lady approaches a hero's son
—Poor child, are you hungry?
—Yes, I am hungry.
—Do you want bread?
—I do not want your bread. I prefer my hunger.
I do not want bread from my father's murderers.
—Rebellious child. I am charity. I forgive you.

—No acepto su perdón ni esas caridades que dan espasmos de placer
a la piel sádica
Prefiero mi hambre y el estruendo de mi lengua moribunda.

Hay un olor a sangre en las llanuras
Laureles para las frentes que se deshacen
Laureles para los héroes proletarios y los hijos de los héroes
Oh camaradas, oh cicatrices y epopeyas de la revolución
Seréis vengados,
Serán vengados vuestros hijos
Esos hijos que se llevan los amos tan caritativos
A colegios de frailes y de aliados oscuros
(Último escarnio a vuestro nombre)
A esos colegios a donde se fabrican seres mansos
Donde se castran leones
Y también se preparan nuevos explotados
Seréis vengados niños de las Asturias
Hijos de esos mineros cuyos pechos estallan en banderas de fuego
Vosotros sois el rayo sorprendido en su raíz
Sois el futuro rugir de los océanos
Y nadie puede acallar el dolor de vuestros siglos
Seréis vengados camaradas
La tiranía caerá de sus torres en cenizas
Se romperán las trabas al paso del designio

Y hay un olor a sangre en Cataluña
Y la sangre viviente va abriéndose un camino,
Un inmenso camino de presagios y cantos
España se despierta en ropas de huracán
Frente a la emboscada del traidor frente al galope mercenario.
España, ahí está el cobarde de costumbres subterráneas
Míralo con todos tus incendios, con tus campos en harapos.
Y hay un olor a sangre en las vertiendes andaluzas
Hay un olor a sangre en la Castilla
Y en todas tus provincias
Y la sangre camina
Y la tierra vio andar hombres vestidos de fuego como lanzas

—I do not accept your forgiveness nor charity that gives spasms of
    pleasure to sadistic skin
I prefer my hunger and the clamour of my dying tongue.

There is a smell of blood on the plains
Laurels for shattered brows
Laurels for proletarian heroes and the children of heroes
Oh comrades, oh scars and epic tales of the revolution
You shall be avenged,
Your children shall be avenged
Those children taken away by such benevolent masters
To schools run by clerics and their shady allies
(Final mockery of your name)
To those schools where they manufacture docile beings
Where lions are castrated
And a new exploited class is prepared
You shall be avenged children of Asturias
Sons of those miners whose chests erupt in banners of fire
You are the lightning bolt revealed in their roots
You are the future roar of oceans
And no one can silence the pain of your centuries
You shall be avenged comrades
Tyranny will fall from its towers in ashes
Bonds will shatter under the tread of destiny

And there is a smell of blood in Catalonia
And living blood is carving a path,
An immense path of omens and songs
Spain awakens clad in hurricanes
Facing the traitor's ambush facing the galloping mercenaries.
Spain, there stands the coward with his subterranean ways
Look upon him with all your fires, with your fields in tatters.
And there is a smell of blood in the gutters of Andalusia
There is a smell of blood in Castille
And in all your provinces
And the blood runs
And the earth saw men walk clothed in fire like spears

Vestidos de montaña de futuro y de mar.
Camaradas españoles
Hay una selva en marcha cantando vuestros nombres
Hay un astro sudando vuestra gloria por sus poros.
Martirio de los mártires
¿Dónde hallar un silencio tan grande para tanta amargura,
Y un himno suficiente a tanta gloria?
Pero hay un mundo infame que agoniza
Y un mundo limpio que se decide a salir de vuestro pecho
Y entonces la tierra escucha esos épicos pasos
Vuestros enormes pasos de montaña de esperanza y de mar
Y la tierra contempla vuestros ojos en la noche
Como esas fogatas de terrible silueta

Cambiarán el mundo los que no tienen alegría sobre el mundo.

Camaradas
La voz de las ciudades
La voz de las llanuras
No hay tiranía que la aplaste
Ni sombra para tan altos signos
Esas miles de heridas
Son un río de lámparas señalando el destino

Hay un olor a sangre en todas España
Y esa sangre será la savia del mañana.

Clothed in mountains of the future and the sea.
Spanish comrades
There is a forest on the march singing your names
There is a star sweating your glory through its pores.
Martyrdom of martyrs
Where can silence vast enough for such bitterness be found,
Or a hymn fitting for such glory?
But there is a despicable world in its death throes
And a pure world deciding to emerge from your chest
And then the earth hears those epic footsteps
Your huge mountain-like steps of hope and sea
And the earth beholds your eyes in the night
Like those bonfires with terrible silhouettes

Those who have no joy in the world will change the world.

Comrades
The voice of the cities
The voice of the plains
No tyranny can crush it
No shadow veils such lofty symbols
Those thousands of wounds
Are a river of lanterns pointing towards destiny

All over Spain there is a smell of blood
And that blood will be the sap of tomorrow.

GLORIA Y SANGRE

Como huracán erguido
Como lágrima rodando por la tierra
Con su luz interior que nada puede apagar
Como anhelo cayendo a través de los siglos hasta hacerse estatua
Como brazo de hierro hirviendo
Como puño condensando edades furibundas
Como sangre España como sangre
Sangre de la Historia devuelta a su cauce de campanas
Sangre de madre sangre de raíz herida de semilla
He ahí el futuro
He ahí el mar saltando en rosas sobre el horizonte
He ahí el sueño besando tu frente España
Besando tu dolor
Y tu alegría de inmensa alumbradora

Permítenos llorar
Que tu heroísmo se haga blando un instante
Lloramos de orgullo repentino
De ternura que no fue elegida como flor
Tenemos el pecho hinchado de tantas tempestades
De tantas esperanzas suspendidas
De tanta alondra arrebatada a su destino

He ahí España
Nombre del porvenir naciendo en llamaradas
Ésa es España
Ardiendo en ramos de mañana y cantos de vidente
Ésa es España
Exhalada en arrebatos de volcanes injuriados
Llevada en hombros de águilas de cielo en cielo
Ésa es España
Camino que sube y se abre en alba persistente

GLORY AND BLOOD

Like an upright hurricane
Like a tear rolling over the earth
With its inner light that nothing can extinguish
Like a yearning that falls through the centuries to become a statue
Like an iron arm seething
Like a fist condensing furious ages
Like blood Spain like blood
Blood of History returned to its channelled bells
A mother's blood blood from wounded roots from seeds
There lies the future
There is the sea leaping in roses over the horizon
There is the dream kissing your brow Spain
Kissing your pain
And your immense illuminating joy

Allow us to weep
Let your heroism soften for a moment
We weep with sudden pride
With tenderness that was not chosen like a flower
Our chests are swollen with so many storms
With so many suspended hopes
With so many larks snatched from their fates

Behold Spain
The name of the future born in flames
That is Spain
Burning in the branches of tomorrow and a seer's songs
That is Spain
Exhaled in eruptions of ill-treated volcanoes
Carried on the shoulders of eagles from sky to sky
That is Spain
A path that climbs and opens onto persistent dawn

Déjanos llorar un poco porque hay tanto que decir
El corazón maduro tiene sus puertas
Tiene sus ríos con plenitudes transitorias
Tiene sus derechos adquiridos sobre los ojos predispuestos
Tiene sus mares y sus ahogados inconsolables
En busca de una estrella que encontraron en el aire
Y que era de ellos como promesa y sueño

La voz tiembla bajo sus ropas
Qué hacer entonces para apoyar el heroísmo

Tiembla en su viaje mojada entre relámpagos
Y al tocar tu frente de insigne parturienta
Entre racimos de astros y tiempos en camino
Estalla en árboles de fuego y rompe sus límites visibles

Déjanos llorar los muertos que tú cantas y te cantan
Déjanos llorar el derrumbe de los huesos
Que se rehacen al horizonte en arcos luminosos
Para esperar el día que todos esperamos
Déjanos llorar tu gloria renacida
España que sube el tono al universo
Y desata los cantos como sol entrañable
España en todo lugar
Ocupando los espacios entre paloma y astro
Viviente en todas partes
En todo corazón en todo aliento y toda quemadura de pecho
Como aire respirado
Aire de presagios y carbones heroicos
Déjanos llorar de tanta gloria recién nacida
Balbuciendo murmullos abriendo los ojos sobre nuestras rodillas
Quién no es madre ante el muerto lleno de lágrimas
Y el niño que sonríe
España de fuego y de destino
Fuego al servicio del destino introducido en la montaña
Que mis ojos te miren
Como ese arroyo que allá lejos se convierte en héroe

Let us weep a little for there is so much to say
The mature heart has its doors
Has its rivers with fleeting fullness
Has its vested rights over ready eyes
Has its seas and its inconsolable drowned men
Searching for a star they found in the air
A star that was theirs like a promise and a dream

The voice trembles beneath its garments
What can be done then to support heroism

It shivers on its journey wet between flashes of lightning
And when it touches your distinguished brow giving birth
Amid clusters of stars and approaching times
It bursts into trees of fire and breaks its visible boundaries

Leave us to mourn the dead you sing of and who sing of you
Leave us to mourn the crumbling bones
That reassemble on the horizon in luminous arches
Awaiting the day that we all await
Leave us to mourn your reborn glory
Spain raising its voice to the universe
And unleashing songs like an affectionate sun
Spain everywhere
Filling the spaces between dove and star
Alive everywhere
In every heart in every breath and every burning bosom
Like air breathed
Air of omens and heroic embers
Let us weep for so much newborn glory
Murmuring softly opening its eyes upon our knees
Who is not a mother before a dead man full of tears
And a child who smiles
Spain of fire and destiny
Fire in the service of destiny nestled in the mountains
May my eyes see you
Like that distant stream turning into a hero

He ahí el futuro saliendo de su herida
El pulso de los bosques entonados y proféticos
El barco de la gran aventura dominando sus olas
La bandera de pájaros que llegan de regiones increíbles
He ahí España entre abrazos y cánticos y sonido de sangre
Ese dulce sonido del mito que se torna en espiga
He ahí la ruta que sube hacia el milagro
He ahí un planeta empujado por hombres hacia el amanecer

There lies the future emerging from its wound
The pulse of haughty and prophetic forests
The ship of great adventure mastering its waves
The banner of birds arriving from incredible realms
There lies Spain amongst embraces and chants and the sound of blood
That sweet sound of myth turning into wheat
There lies the path leading up to the miracle
There lies a planet pushed by mankind towards dawn

ESPAÑA

Traidores nocturnos con alma pantanosa
Hermanos de la víbora y las ropas de luto
Apuñalaron tu hermosa estrella esperanzada
Entre algas y tinieblas entre ríos difuntos

Sopla el mar fabricando pirámides de lágrimas
Fatales escaleras y músicas con sangre
Bajo nubes que pasan como carros de heridos
Por un cielo color turbio de cañones distantes

La epopeya del pueblo que exige su destino
Levanta al cielo frentes y rompe grandes pechos
Y danzan los fantasmas entre barcos enfermos
En la noche del hombre que nutre cementerios

Pasan soldados pasan olas y pasan vientos

Como notas de un canto que asusta a las edades
La inmensa sinfonía con su lluvia y sus hombres
Se pierde en una tumba debajo de la tarde

Ejércitos de luces al borde de la muerte
Se alza la selva y los soldados pasan en su canto
Es el gran viaje ciego de las velas y el viento
Y a no veréis más esos soldados

Una fila tras otra asaltan horizontes
Y vienen a morir en olas a la playa
Tanta sonrisa tanta sangre tantos héroes que caen
Y salen de sus cuerpos como salían de las fábricas

El recuerdo del hombre es menos que esa luna
Que pierde la cabeza y cae sobre el mar

SPAIN

Nocturnal traitors with swampy souls
Brothers of the viper and in mourning dress
They stabbed your beautiful hopeful star
Amongst seaweed and shadows amongst dead rivers

The sea blows making pyramids of tears
Fatal stairways and blood-soaked music
Beneath clouds passing like carts bearing the wounded
Through a sky murky with the smoke of distant cannon

The epic tale of people demanding their destiny
Raises foreheads to the heavens and breaks open great chests
And phantoms dance amongst sickly ships
In the night of the man who feeds cemeteries

Soldiers pass by, waves pass by, and winds pass by

Like notes of a song that frightens the ages
The immense symphony with its rain and its people
Fades into a grave beneath the dusk

Armies of light on the brink of death
The forest stirs and the soldiers march to its song
It is the great blind voyage of sails and wind
And you will see those soldiers no more

One column after another they assault horizons
And come to die in waves upon the shore
So many smiles so much blood so many falling heroes
And they rise from their bodies as they once rose from the factories

Mankind's memory is less than that moon
Which loses its head and falls upon the sea

Sin embargo esos rostros de soldados que pasan
Ya nunca los podréis olvidar

Agonía agonía de la rosa y la piedra

Los vientos se estrellaron en la más alta torre
Caerán mil estrellas con la quilla partida
Y cada una en la tierra tendrá más de cien nombres

El pueblo será grande como su propia estatua
Como ese continente que sacó de la noche
Como el galope histórico de épicas mesnadas
Que dan escalofríos a las alas del bosque

Laureles y laureles y cien leones antiguos
Petrificados por el rayo y los relámpagos
Procesión de ataúdes en puentes al silencio
La libertad bien vale un astro emocionado

Y pasan los fantasmas atados por la sombra
Laureles y laureles y truenos y relámpagos
Y vienen los lamentos y los ramos de gloria
Ya no podréis jamás olvidar esos soldados

Sus esqueletos vivos debajo de la tierra
Serán los clavecines de una música eterna

Yet the faces of those passing soldiers
You will never forget them

Agony agony of rose and stone

The winds struck the highest tower
A thousand stars will fall with broken keels
And each one upon the earth will bear more than a hundred names

The people will grow as large as their own statue
Like that continent that they brought out of the night
Like the historic charge of epic bands
That sends shivers through the wings of the forest

Laurels upon laurels and a hundred ancient lions
Petrified by the flashes and lightning
A procession of coffins on bridges to the silence
Freedom is well worth an excited star

And phantoms pass by bound by shadows
Laurels upon laurels and thunder and lightning
And lamentations come with bouquets of glory
You will never forget those soldiers

Their living skeletons beneath the earth
Will be the harpsichords of a timeless music

PASIONARIA

Vas con tu voz de alma abierta en rosas
Vas en tu voz a todos los dolores y todas las esperanzas
Y llenas de madre el mundo
Te deshojas en fe y en entusiasmo y en piedad
Tus pétalos cierran las heridas
Y perfuman las lágrimas tan huérfanas como la pluma que se cayó de
una gaviota al mar
Vas con tu voz y tus pétalos dulces
Vas haciendo nidos con tu mirada llena de ángeles
Vas vestida de gloria junto a la muerte coronando muertos
Vas vestida de fuego junto a la vida despertando vida
Llegas primero como noticia de alba
Como nacer de un niño sobre miles de brazos extendidos
Llegas como el barco que trae tesoros y luz de islas remotas
Y rumores de grandes ríos en lucha con océanos feroces
Es preciso sacudir al cielo
Y despertar los mares y decirles todo lo que está pasando
Es preciso informar a las estrellas cuando bajan más cerca
O cuando una voz sube más alta
Hora es que el destino se haga carne y cálido prodigio
Tierra nuestra tierra España Pasionaria
Voz visible como inscripción de sueño
Voz en forma de luz ansiosa
En forma de agua para la sed y de pan para el hambre
De dolor de los siglos pasados
Para crear la alegría de los siglos futuros
Mujer de España labio de las tierras ofendidas
España en carne y nido y árbol
De qué honduras vienen tus escalofríos
Qué molinos de viento se hicieron arco-iris
Y qué alas batían el tiempo en tu garganta
Para que no se sintiera su dureza
Eres el hada de corazón interminable

PASIONARIA

You walk with your voice of an open soul in roses
Your voice carries with it all pains and all hopes
And you fill the world with motherhood
You shed yourself in faith and enthusiasm and compassion
Your petals close the wounds
And perfume your tears orphaned just like a feather falling from a seagull
into the sea
You walk with your voice and your sweet petals
You build nests with your gaze full of angels
You walk beside death dressed in glory crowning the fallen
You walk beside life dressed in fire awakening life
You arrive first like the announcement of dawn
Like the birth of a child cradled in thousands of outstretched arms
You arrive like a ship bringing treasures and light from remote islands
And rumours of great rivers battling with ferocious oceans
The sky needs to be shaken
And the seas to be awakened and told all that is happening
The stars need to be told when they draw closer
Or when a voice rises higher
Now is the time for destiny to become flesh and a warm miracle
Our land our Spain Pasionaria
A visible voice like a dream written down
A voice in the form of eager light
In the form of water for thirst and bread for hunger
Of suffering from centuries past
To create the joy of centuries still to come
Woman of Spain lips of offended lands
Spain made flesh and nest and tree
From what depths do your shivers rise
What windmills turned into rainbows
And what wings beat time in your throat
So its harshness would not be felt
You are the sprite with an endless heart

Eres la cuna de las edades luminosas trepando al horizonte
Vas tan serena con tu destino a cuestas y tantos otros destinos
Sobre un camino de sangre con tu canasta de plumas suaves
Allí donde se mezcla la muerte con la vida
Apareces y estrujas tus racimos sobre las bocas de piedra comenzada
Tiendes las alas y sonríes de ternura sobre los ojos que van a hacerse
          estrellas de su gloria
Qué viento de muerte absorbes

Qué viento de vida exhalas
Mujer con la garganta llena de paisajes doloridos
Mujer de tierra firme y cielos hinchados de optimismo
Mujer de terciopelo y armaduras
Naciendo en cada ensueño visible en toda herida
Cruzada de palomas y de truenos
Vas y te acercas y todas las alas llegan
Y todas las bocas cantan en la marea que sube
El dolor de los tiempos pasados
Para crear la alegría de los tiempos futuros

You are the cradle of luminous ages climbing towards the horizon
You walk so serenely bearing your destiny and that of so many others
On a path of blood with your basket of soft feathers
There where death mingles with life
You appear and squeeze your grapes above the stone mouths just forming
You spread your wings and smile tenderly at eyes that are destined to
become stars in their own glory
What winds of death you swallow

What winds of life you breathe out
Woman whose throat is filled with grieving landscapes
Woman of solid earth and skies swollen with optimism
Woman of velvet and armour
Being born in every visible dream in every wound
Crusader of doves and thunder
You walk and you come closer and all the wings come with you
And with the rising tide all mouths sing of
The pain of times past
To create the joy of times to come

FUERA DE AQUÍ

¿Qué buscáis en esta tierra aviadores fascistas
Fantasmas de la muerte que habéis falsificado vuestra Italia
La cuna de piel tibia que os ofreció la vida?
¿Qué buscáis en esta tierra os pregunto criminales sangrientos
asesinos de niños españoles?
Vuestro paseo por América ¿es insolencia o es demencia?
Salid de nuestras tierras, salid de estas montañas limpias que saben
hablar con las estrellas
Fuera de Chile, fuera de América, asesinos, corazones podridos
No vengáis a manchar nuestros paisajes con el olor a sangre que
despiden vuestras manos
Sangre de niños españoles, sangre de España, sangre nuestra que
nosotros besamos, que nosotros amamos y bendecimos
Sangre que se prolonga en nuestras venas, sangre que viene de nuestras
madres y va a nuestros hijos
Sangre sublime que crea continentes, sangre de España, sangre de madre
inagotable, sangre que nosotros adoramos de rodillas
Fuera, fuera de aquí
¿Es insolencia o es demencia?
Comerciantes de la muerte, animales geológicos de nocturno aullido,
mi tierra no es burdel ni es una caverna ni la deseamos
cementerio
Fuera de aquí pájaros de mal agüero, aves de rapiña que hasta el cielo
ponéis hediondo.
Valientes frente a niños que lloran y mujeres indefensas, héroes frente a
pueblos sin armas. Sois el vértigo de la fuga apenas un árbol se
equivoca y hace ruido de bombarda
Sois una ofensa a la auténtica Italia, sois la deshonra del hombre, la
negación del tiempo transcurrido, sois la vuelta al dolmen, al
mono de las tinieblas, a la bestia al acecho.
Fuera de nuestras tierras sagradas hoy por ser hijos de España
¿Es insolencia o es demencia?

GET OUT OF HERE

What do you fascist aviators seek in this land?
Phantoms of death who have perverted your Italy
That warm fur cradle that once gave you life?
What do you seek in this land I ask you you bloodstained criminals you murderers of Spanish children?
Is your passage through America born of insolence or of insanity?
Leave our land, leave these clean mountains that can speak to the stars
Get out of Chile, get out of America, murderers, rotten hearts
Do not come and stain our landscape with the stench of blood that drips from your hands
Blood of Spanish children, blood of Spain, our blood that we kiss, that we love and we bless
Blood that flows through our veins, blood that comes from our mothers and passes on to our children
Sublime blood that creates continents, blood of Spain, blood of an inexhaustible mother, blood we adore on our knees
Get out, get out of here
Is this insolence or is it insanity?
Merchants of death, geological beasts that howl by night, my land is no brothel nor is it a cavern nor do we wish to make of it a cemetery
Get out of here you birds of ill omen, birds of prey that make even the sky stink.
Brave only when faced with crying children and defenceless women, heroes when faced by unarmed people. You flee with dizzying speed as soon as you confuse the sound of trees for that of a bomber
You are an insult to the real Italy, you dishonour mankind, you are a denial of the progress of time, you are the return to dolmens, to the ape in the darkness, to lurking beasts.
Get out of our sacred lands today for we are children of Spain
Is this insolence or is it insanity?

Nuestros pueblos os maldicen porque llegáis chorreando sangre de niños, madres que viven en nuestros pechos
Levantaos pueblos de América y expulsad a los siniestros búhos de la tribu difunta
No humillaréis nuestros ríos que cantan a España en su misma lengua con un acento un poco más montañoso. No humillaréis nuestras selvas que son una alabanza trémula a su historia. No ensuciaréis los vientos de América. No injuriaréis nuestros paisajes colocados por el sol.
Al fondo de vuestros ojos hay pequeñas vísceras destrozadas, carne de pétalos llenos de promesas, hay piececitos cortados que apenas ensayaban andar sobre su tierra, hay manitas que aplaudían al sol en las mañanas, hay bocas en la horrible mueca final anticipada por vuestros heroicos aviones, bocas entre dos hilos de sangre cuyo recuerdo se levantará ante vosotros el día de vuestra muerte, hay labios de beso y leche que sólo sabían decir madre y no alcanzaron siquiera a llamar a sus madres, labios que iban a cantar la vida cuando vosotros los tremendos valientes cortasteis a la vida.
Aguiluchos de nubes sanguinarias
Subían por el cielo a enlodar el cielo, a poner fétido el aire con su aliento de sepulcros y caballos desenterrados
Pasaban sobre ciudades indefensas y sembraban la muerte en la inocencia y en las casas hinchadas y dejaban las paredes gimiendo y un mar de miembros aprendices saltando en olas desesperadas
¿Por qué? Decid ¿por qué? ¿Por qué? ¿Por qué? gritaban las madres girando enloquecidas en torno a su dolor ¿Por qué? ¿Por qué?
¿Quién os mandaba allí con qué derecho metíais vuestra infamia en esas tierras pletóricas de verdaderos heroísmos, de verdaderas epopeyas?
¿Qué envidia impulsaba vuestros motores trágicos y vuestras almas oscuras?
¿Quién os metía allí peleles miserables, teatro de calaveras espantadas de sus sombras, corazones arrugados, piernas eléctricas de fuga?
Y ahora ¿quién os manda aquí?
Decid al gran pelele, vuestro jefe, vuestro grotesco Duce que puede tomar actitudes napoleónicas frente a todos los espejos, imitar a los césares en tarjetas postales, no impedirá que oigamos crujir el proscenio bajo sus plantas.

Our people curse you because you come drenched in the blood of
children, of mothers who live in our hearts
Rise up peoples of America and drive out these sinister owls from an
extinct tribe
You will not humiliate our rivers that sing to Spain in its own tongue
with a slightly more mountainous accent. You will not
humiliate our forests that are a tremulous eulogy to her history.
You will not befoul the winds of America. You will not abuse
our landscapes set there by the sun.
In the depths of your eyes lie shredded viscera, flesh of petals once full of
promise, there are tiny severed feet that had barely begun to
walk the land, there are tiny hands that clapped in the morning
sun, there are mouths in the hideous final grimace brought on
by your heroic planes, mouths with trickles of blood the
memory of which will rise up before you the day you die, lips
with kisses and milk that knew only how to say mother and
never even managed to call out to their mothers, lips that were
meant to sing of life until you in your terrible bravery cut short
their lives.
Hawks in bloodstained clouds
They rose up through the sky to befoul the heavens, to poison the air with
the stench of graves and exhumed horses
They passed over defenceless cities sowing death amongst the innocent
and on crowded homes leaving walls groaning and a sea of
desperate limbs leaping like waves
Why? Tell me why? Why? Why? the mothers cry out, whirling around
madly in their grief? Why? why?
Who sent you there? By what right did you bring your infamy to those
lands filled with real heroism, and genuine epic tales?
What envy drove your tragic engines and your dark souls?
Who sent you there you wretched puppets, theatre of skulls frightened
by their own shadows, shrivelled hearts, legs electric with the
need to flee?
And now, who sends you here?
Tell the great scarecrow, your boss, your grotesque Duce he can strike
Napoleonic poses in front of all the mirrors, mimic Caesar on
postcards, but that will not prevent us from hearing the stage
creaking beneath his feet.

Fuera de aquí los monstruos, fuera con la sangre chorreando de las manos, con las orejas llenas de alaridos infantiles ascendiendo y el clamor de millones de gargantas maternales, ese clamor que dejará temblando las noches de la tierra y los gemidos mutilados en mar y en universo sin consuelo.
¿Es insolencia o es demencia?
Fuera de aquí aviadores fascistas somos hijos de España, su dolor es molido en nuestro pecho, su victoria será arco-iris en nuestras almas.
Llevamos como una flor enorme el orgullo de sentirnos españoles.
Despreciamos vuestros ojos de buscadores de muerte, vuestra mirada de metralla ansiosa.
(Primero os aseguráis que vuestras víctimas no estén armadas y luego acometéis. Héroes de una epopeya de conejos en delirio. Despreciamos vuestras piernas de fuga, vuestras manos con ruido de chacales lejanos.)
Fuera de aquí en nombre de nuestras madres y sus hermanas muertas, fuera de aquí en nombre de nuestros hijos y de sus hermanos muertos. Fuera de aquí en nombre de la cultura, en nombre de la dignidad de ser humanos
Fuera de Chile en nombre de los chilenos, fuera de América en nombre de todos los americanos que sienten el honor de los más vastos horizontes y comprenden la voz de su profundo origen.
Fuera de aquí extranjeros de nuestra tierra, extranjeros del mundo, extranjeros del hombre.
Esto también es España
Aquí está España, estará España mientras haya hombres cuyo pecho se agranda al sentir sus raíces. ¡España! Este nombre os aplasta, os revuelca en medio de la historia.
Fuera de aquí. ¿Es insolencia o es demencia?
Os odio os aborrezco seres sin luz, os odio porque España es mía y yo soy de ella, porque sus niños están creciendo en mi garganta y son un gemido que se convierte en maldición. Os odio por todos los muertos que habéis echado en mis espaldas, os odio en nombre de mis muertos.
Corazones de estiércol llorad si sois capaces todavía, llorad por esos piececitos que llenaban de gracia el mundo, llorad por esas pequeñas voces que corrían por el aire como globos azules, llorad por esas bocas de beso y leche, de fruta y flor, llorad por el entierro

Get out of here you monsters, get out with your hands dripping with
blood, your ears full of rising children's screams and the clamour
of millions of motherly throats, a clamour that will leave nights
on earth trembling and a mutilated lament spreading over the
seas and an inconsolable universe.
Is this insolence or is it insanity?
Get out of here you fascist aviators we are the children of Spain, her pain
is ground into our hearts, her victory will be a rainbow in our souls.
We carry the pride of being Spanish as if it were a huge flower.
We despise your death-seeking eyes, your gaze of greedy shrapnel.
(First you make sure your victims are unarmed and then you attack.
Heroes from an epic of deluded rabbits. We despise your fleeing
legs, your hands with the sounds of distant jackals.)
Get out of here in the name of our mothers and their dead sisters, get
out of here in the name of our sons and their dead brothers.
Get out of here in the name of culture, in the name of human
dignity.
Get out of Chile in the name of all Chileans, get out of America in the
name of all Americans who feel the honour of its vast horizons
and understand the voice of their profound origins.
Get out of here, strangers to our land, strangers to the world, strangers
to humanity.
This too is Spain
Here is Spain, here Spain will be as long as there are men whose hearts
swell when feeling their roots. Spain! This name crushes you,
it tramples you in the midst of history.
Get out of here. Is this insolence or is it insanity?
I hate you I loathe you beings without light, I hate you because Spain
is mine and I am hers, because her children are growing in my
throat and their cries turn into curses. I hate you for all the
dead you have placed upon my shoulders, I hate you in the name
of my dead.
You dung-filled hearts weep if you are still able, weep for those little feet
that filled the world with grace, weep for those little voices that
floated through the air like blue balloons, weep for those lips of
kisses and milk, of fruit and flowers, weep for the burial of the

de la tierra, por el cielo enlutado, llorad por los árboles llorando,
llorad por todas las madres que son una inmensa lágrima
Id a ocultaros bajo la tierra, cavad vuestra tumba en un barro de escupos.
No hay suficiente lápida para vosotros. Echaos encima los Andes
y el Himalaya. No hay suficiente lápida para cubrir vuestra
ignominia.
Al fondo del planeta, en el último abismo de este astro desgraciado
porque vosotros lo habitáis en el más profundo rincón, bajo
siete océanos, hasta el último siglo oiréis la maldición del hombre.

earth, for the sky in mourning, weep for the weeping trees, weep
for all the mothers who are one enormous tear
Go and hide away beneath the earth, dig your grave in mud and phlegm.
There is no tombstone large enough for you. Lay yourselves down
on top of the Andes and the Himalayas. There are no tombstones
large enough to cover your infamy.
Deep inside the planet, in the final abyss of this orb that you disgrace
by dwelling upon it, in its farthest corner, beneath seven oceans,
you will hear the curses of humanity until the end of time.

TCHU-DE

Era suya la estrella y se la trajo el viento
En las llanuras chinas donde golpeaban contra su pecho
Porque era el jefe de mirar de lenguas sorprendidas
Recto ancestral como su gran muralla ya casi de carne de la tierra
General del Ejército Rojo del dolor de los siglos
Rojo de ansias solares de estruendo de manos libertadas
Con sus oídos de torre hacia las lejanías
Con sus sentidos de vigía y de ventana abierta
Como piedra salida de su invierno
Y su voz de mando para romper cadenas
Y derrumbar muros injustos y llenar la tierra de semillas alegres

Qué de espaldas de montaña habituada a los astros
Qué sólidos cimientos para el día del hombre
Qué costumbre de rayo para las tropas rojas
Invencible como un cometa que va arrastrando al cielo
Capitán
Capitán del destino
Tanta tortura tanta muerte
Hizo brotar el rayo

Capitán de millones de anhelos
Que han sabido hacerse hombres como el arroyo río
Capitán del espíritu en marcha hacia la vida
Todos los volcanes del Asia te saludan
Cómo te veneramos en nuestra noche a la puerta de la esperanza
Como los tuyos te veneran y todos los brotes de la noche
Y los mares entusiastas y las hierbas de buena voluntad
Capitán del destino presuroso
Frente a un clima a sangre y fuego
Levantas tu infatigable sol apoyado en la vida
Frente al llanto del tiempo

ZHU DE

The star was his and the wind brought it to him
On the Chinese plains where they beat against his chest
For he was the leader the watcher of startled tongues
Ancestrally upright like his great wall now almost flesh of the earth
General of the Red Army with the pain of the ages
Red with solar yearnings with the roar of liberated hands
With ears like towers tuned to distant lands
Alert senses on the lookout like an open window
Like a stone emerging from its winter
And his word of command to break the chains
And tear down unjust walls and fill the earth with joyful seeds

What mountainous shoulders accustomed to the stars
What solid foundations for the day of mankind
What familiarity with lightning for the red troops
Invincible as a comet sweeping across the sky
Captain
Captain of destiny
So much torture so much death
Brought forth the lightning

Captain of millions of desires
That have learned to become men as streams become rivers
Captain of the spirit on the march towards life
All the volcanoes of Asia salute you
How we revere you during our night by the gates of hope
As your people revere you and all the fresh shoots of the night
And the enthusiastic seas and the grasses of goodwill
Captain of swift destiny
Facing a climate of blood and fire
You raise your tireless sun supported by life
Facing the weeping of time

Frente al furor de lobos calculados
Levantas tu selva de pedestal humano

Capitán del presente vestido de flores tempestuosas
Eres la suma de siglos dolores y miserias
Interminable derrumbe de huesos
Que se levantan al fin en monumento

Eres el trueno que hace morder la lluvia al enemigo
El enemigo sin costumbres de grandes sueños
Y en alianza perpetua con la muerte
O Capitán de mañana llegado en imperiosa luz
Dictado en profecías y con ese horno de destinos sin llanto
Aquí estamos frente a las olas de un mismo mar
A través del Pacífico y sus aguas alzadas contra la noche
Estrechamos tus manos que son lámpara y vida
Vida en tumulto y fuego de nuevas profecías
Capitán entre campanas de juventud y pechos en hoguera
Eres el triunfo amaneciendo sobre el astro que amanece
Eres el triunfo repartido en eco a todos los confines

Facing the fury of calculated wolves
You raise your forest on a human pedestal

Captain of the present clad in stormy flowers
You are the sum of centuries of pain and misery
Endlessly crumbling bones
That are finally raised as a monument

You are the thunder that makes the rain bite your enemies
The enemy without any tradition of grand dreams
And forever allied with death
Oh Captain of tomorrow arriving in imperious light
Proclaimed in prophecies and with that furnace of destiny without tears
Here we are facing the waves of the same sea
Across the Pacific its waters rising against the night
We clasp your hands that are lanterns and life
Life in tumult and fire with new prophecies
Captain amidst bells of youth and hearts aflame
You are the triumph dawning on the dawn star
You are the triumph echoing to the ends of the earth

CANTO A FRANCIA

Francia
Tú dormías soñando que lo que habías dado al mundo era suficiente
para hacerte amar.

Tú cantabas sobre nuestros días y sobre nuestras noches inagotablemente
Tú eras la canción de la Tierra que es su canto
Tú dijiste Fraternidad y no te oyeron. Dijiste libertad y se mofaron
Pero tu voz quedó anclada en los pechos más altos
Tu voz ha germinado en las tierras más hondas
Nadie podrá acallar tu voz. Era tan justa, tan sincera, tan humana, y decía
el ansia oscura de los siglos
Ésa es tu grandeza y por eso los pueblos te veneran.
Vencedora o vencida, estarás siempre en el registro más profundo de mi
pecho

Francia.
Una tragedia gigantesca se establece en tus campiñas. Olor de puerta que se
abren en el tiempo. Olor de eternidad y estatua comenzada. Los
muertos prematuros como grandes ojos al fondo del abismo y la
memoria
Los muertos prematuros.

Francia.
Indispensable. ¡Oh, agua, oh, sol de las naciones!
Nuestros pechos están llenos de un sabor de amargura y temblores de
inquietud.
¿Es posible que aún no se comprenda?
Aquí estoy sacudido por tus siglos, traspasado por tus grandes heridas.

El olor de la muerte sube a la punta de los árboles.

Francia.
Tú eres la cordura.

SONG FOR FRANCE

France
You were sleeping dreaming that what you had given to the world was
enough to make you loved.

You sang tirelessly of our days and of our nights
You were the song of the Earth which is its anthem
You said Fraternity and they did not hear you. You said freedom and
they scoffed
But your voice stayed secure in the loftiest hearts
Your voice has germinated in the remotest lands
No one can silence your voice. It was so just, so sincere, so human, and
it spoke of the dark yearning of the ages
That is your greatness and that is why people revere you.
Victorious or vanquished, you will always be inscribed in the deepest part
of my heart

France.
A gigantic tragedy unfolds in your fields. The smell of doors opening onto
time. The smell of eternity and an unfinished statue. Those dead
before their time like big eyes deep in the abyss and in memory
Those dead before their time.

France.
Indispensable. Oh water, oh sun of nations!
Our breasts are filled with a bitter taste and trembling unease.
Can it be that this is still not understood?
Here I am shaken by your centuries, pierced by your great wounds.

The smell of death rises to the treetops.

France.
You are reason.

Tú la relación exacta.
Eres la piedra armoniosa del enigma. El sentido del vivir.
Tú eres la tradición que muere aferrándose a los últimos muros y eres la tradición que nace entre sonrisas y flores entusiastas.
Cuando entras en la noche ¡cuán poco perdura! Con qué facilidad te sale el alba.

Francia.
Los hombres tienen una sombra voraz que los persigue y se los traga.
Los hombres tienen palabras fabulosas que los aplastan. Y mitos que abren millones de tumbas a una voz de mando.
¿Qué apareció en la tierra que pueda olvidarse su grandeza?
¿Quién puede exigir tu muerte?
¿Qué cosa ofrecen otros que tú no hayas ofrecido a través de tus años?
¿Qué apareció en el mundo que valga tu sepulcro?

Francia.
Pienso en mis amigos que mueren o que pueden morir y tiemblo.
Mis amigos, tus mejores poetas. Y se me hincha el corazón.
Pienso en todos tus hijos que por tuyos son también de mi dolor.
Oigo tu voz, André Malraux, oigo la tuya André Breton, te veo aquí ante mí Paul Éluard,
Oigo tu voz de piedra, hermano Jacques, oigo tu voz Hans Arp.
Oídme también vosotros. Tú, André Masson, Roger Vitrac, Pablo Picasso.

¿Qué peligro os acecha? Oídme Daumal, Lecomte, Sima, Dida, Menil, Hélion.
¿No me escucháis? No puedo gritar más. Os amo entrañablemente.
Tanguy, Magritte, Georges Braque, Joë Bousquet y el vieux maître Saint-Pol Roux y Henri Matisse y André Derain.
Estoy temblando, Francia. ¡Oh, esponja de vinagre en los labios temblando!

Francia.
El olor de la muerte sube a las copas de los árboles.
Todos tus ríos desembocan en mi corazón.
Aquí, en mi pecho, siento las raíces de tu tierra y tu lección de altura iluminada.

You are the precise balance.
You are the riddle's harmonic stone. The meaning of life.
You are the tradition that dies clinging to the last walls and you are the tradition being born amongst smiles and enthusiastic flowers.
When you enter the night how briefly it lasts! How easily the dawn breaks over you.

France.
Men have a ravenous shadow that hunts them down and devours them.
Men carry fabulous words that crush them. And myths that open millions of graves with a commanding voice.
What has the earth created that could erase their greatness?
Who can demand your death?
What do others offer that you have not offered throughout your years?
What has the world created that is worth your grave?

France.
I think of my friends who are dying or who might die and I tremble.
My friends, your finest poets. And my heart overflows.
I think of all your children who, because they are yours, are my pain too.
I hear your voice, André Malraux, I hear yours André Breton, I see you here before me Paul Éluard,
I hear your stony voice, brother Jacques, I hear your voice Hans Arp.
Hear me all of you. You, André Masson, Roger Vitrac, Pablo Picasso.

What danger lies in wait for you? Hear me Daumal, Lecomte, Sima, Dida, Menil, Hélion.
Can you not hear me? I cannot shout any louder. I love you dearly.
Tanguy, Magritte, Georges Braque, Joë Bousquet and the old master Saint-Pol Roux and Henri Matisse and André Derain.
I am trembling, France. Oh, sponge with vinegar on my trembling lips!

France.
The smell of death rises to the treetops.
All your rivers empty into my heart.
Here, in my chest, I feel the roots of your land and your lessons in enlightened excellence.

Si el rostro de la grandeza rueda por los caminos, tú los has de recoger.
Sobre tus hombros nunca será una máscara.

Francia.
Tu pueblo de truenos conoce su hora y las horas del silencio y las horas de espera y la hora de cada cual y su justicia.
Es verdad, tú eres el pecho de los tiempos.
Tus ciudades hirviendo, tus caminos de tanta historia, donde pasaron los tropeles de siglos resonando, las trenzas de las hadas, las armaduras, las estrellas, los caballos que saludan estornudando, los entierros de hombres estatuarios en sueños de crespones y estandartes.
Los siglos, las edades.
Las hojas cayendo.
Hombres con deseos de matar, contempla, y que tus manos se anuden con ramas colgadas sobre el mar.

Francia.
¡Qué ruido de enormes ruedas!
Colinas sollozando, ciudades lavando sus heridas en el río.
Campamentos oscuros. ¡Oh, niños tristes en sus rosas inseguras!
Y los que han muerto y los que van a morir.
Y los que avanzan en columnas cerradas y los que van buscando su estrella.
Acaso estamos en el umbral de una gran cosa que anuncia felicidad entre tambores dolorosos y el viento de la noche.

Francia.
El olor de la muerte sube sube a las más altas hojas de los árboles.
¿En qué pedazo tuyo de trigos verdes va a morir también mi adolescencia?
Mi adolescencia. Mi niñez. ¡Aquellos años!
Ah, qué ríos inquietos. Con cuánta razón te di mi adolescencia.
Ah, qué olas en su fuerza, qué brisas en el alba en relación a los cantares.

Dulzura. Luz pegada a la frente.
Instante adivinatorio de mano en mano.
Antorcha, amor. Barcos de amor temblando en lejanías al fondo del sueño.

If the face of greatness falls by the wayside, you are there to pick it up.
Upon your shoulders it will never be a mask.

France.
Your people of thunder know their hour and the silent hours and the
hours of waiting and each individual's hour and their justice.
It is true, you are the heart of the ages.
Your cities on the boil, your roads with so much history, where the
centuries trooped by reverberating, braids of fairies, armour, stars,
horses snorting their greetings, the burials of monumental men
in dreams of crests and banners.
Centuries, ages.
Leaves falling.
Men with the urge to kill, think it over, and let your hands entwine with
branches hanging over the sea.

France.
What a noise from those huge wheels!
Hills sobbing, cities washing their wounds in the rivers.
Dark camps. Oh, sad children with their fragile roses!
And those who have died and those who are going to die.
And those who advance in tight ranks and those who search for their star.
Perhaps we stand at the threshold of a great event that promises joy
amidst sad drumbeats and the night wind.

France.
The smell of death rises rises to the highest leaves on the trees.
On what scrap of your green wheat will my youth also die?
My youth. My childhood. Those years!
Ah, what restless rivers. How right I was to give you my youth.
Ah, such powerful waves, such dawn breezes as narrated in epic poems.

Sweetness. Light pressed to the brow.
The prophetic moment passed from one hand to the next.
Firebrand, love. Ships of love trembling far away deep in their dreams.

Francia, mi Francia.
Cosas feroces que sollozan. Mis poemas rayados en tu entraña.
La voz de macho ronco.
Cosas altivas que gimen en su león de alondra.
Y la ternura de las tiernas como puentes a la cumbre. Y los suspiros de palomas suplicantes.
Mi adolescencia. El día dulce y feroz, ¡que no tenga fin!
El barco ardiendo en altamar.

Francia.
Vestida de arroyos temerarios.
Sólo te debo bienes y una riqueza para el alma que puede hacer alianza con la muerte.
De ayer a hoy. Todo lo largo de mi ayer a hoy está tu dulce cuerpo, tu profunda entraña.
¿Te acuerdas de mi primera juventud? Entonces también los hombres morían por la esperanza.
Y un lazo oscuro se ató entre nuestras almas.
Desde entonces soy tuyo y tu dolor es mío.

Francia. Mi Francia.
Exaltación del alma a las últimas cimas.
¿Qué ola de fondo quiere arrastrarte? ¿Qué amante desesperado pretende devorarte en las tinieblas?
Pueblo de hombres tan íntimamente humanos.
Pueblo de fundadores de porvenir.
¿Quién rehará el rostro de la grandeza y lo llevará otra vez en medio de la luz del día?

Francia. Mi Francia.
Te estás hiriendo en mi corazón. Tu sangre me baña el cuerpo.
Crujen mis manos como el odio impotente.

Pasos de fatuidad insultan tu armonía. Galopes de la arrogancia hacen temblar tu tímpano habituado a los ritmos del espíritu.
Pero, encima de la muerte, más allá del dolor, sobre las cabezas amargas de los hombres hay una luz que hace señas y que llama como el relincho de los potros

France, my France.
Fierce things that sob. My poems etched in your heart.
The growling man's voice.
Proud things that whistle like leonine larks.
And the gentility of gentle women like bridges to the summit. And the
sighs of pleading doves.
My youth. The sweet fierce day, may it never end!
The vessel burning on the high seas.

France.
Dressed with reckless streams.
I owe you only land and wealth for the soul that can be allied with death.
From yesterday to today. Right through my yesterday and up until today
there is your sweet body, your profound heart.
Do you remember my early youth? Even then men were dying for hope.
And a dark bond tied our souls together.
Since then I have been yours and your pain is mine.

France. My France.
Exalting the soul to the highest peaks.
What undertow seeks to drag you away? What desperate lover aims to
devour you in the darkness?
A people with men so intimately human.
A people with those who forge the future.
Who will restore the face of greatness and carry it once more into the
light of day?

France. My France.
You are ailing in my heart. Your blood bathes my body.
My hands creak with impotent hatred.

Stupid footsteps insult your harmony. Galloping arrogance shakes your
eardrums accustomed to the rhythms of the spirit.
But, beyond death, beyond pain, above the bitter heads of mankind, there
is a light beckoning and calling like the neighing of stallions

Francia. Mi Francia.
El olor de la muerte sube a sus más audaces árboles.
¿Quién es ese sepulturero furibundo que horada las tierras incansables?
¡Que se cuelgue de una viga!
¿Qué pretenden esos siniestros ojos en medio de sus matorrales?
¿Quién es el gran sepulturero infatigable? ¿De dónde viene? ¿Qué busca?
¿Hacia qué apoteosis de esqueletos quiere arrastrar a los hombres?
¡Ah, que apriete el cañón contra sus sienes y eche a volar los sesos de
rapiña!
Alegría y reposo.

Francia. Mi Francia.
Estás herida. Pero mañana la Historia se pondrá de rodillas.
Mañana, Francia mía, el lobo en su diamante comprenderá tus signos.
El mundo nuevo habrá nacido.
Nacerá del dolor de la más Alta, la más Serena, la más Fuerte.

France. My France.
The smell of death climbs up its boldest trees.
Who is that frenzied gravedigger that penetrated the tireless earth?
May he be hung from a beam!
What are those sinister eyes up to amidst the bushes?
Who is the great tireless gravedigger? Where is he from? What does he
seek?
To what apotheosis of skeletons does he aim to drag men?
Ah, let him press the gun to his temple and blow his rapacious brains out!
Joy and rest.

France. My France.
You are wounded. But tomorrow History will kneel before you.
Tomorrow, my France, the wolf within its diamond will understand
your gestures.
The new world will be born.
It will be born of the pain of the Highest, the Most Serene, the Strongest.

CANTO A LOS SOLDADOS AMERICANOS

Ahí van ahí van
Por el aire por la tierra por el mar
Ahí van los atlantes del Nuevo Mundo
Con un hemisferio a cuestas
A enjugar las lágrimas del otro

Ahí van ahí van
Por el aire que les abre los brazos
Por los mares que se hinchan de orgullo
Por los desiertos de arenas legendarias
Por las montañas

Ahí van ahí van
Bajo el sol implacable que madura los ojos
Sobre la nieve que endulza las heridas
Ahí van los heroicos muchachos
Con su sonrisa abierta al cielo a la tierra y al mar
Ahí van los soldados de tu América Walt Whitman
Ahí van al gran sacrificio de la gloria
Con el amor del mundo en las entrañas

Ahí va el hombre
Con la palabra libertad en medio de la boca
La mágica palabra
Más grande que todas las bocas de la tierra
Más honda que todos los poemas
Más fuerte que todos los volcanes

Ahí va el hombre
Camino de su estatua
A aplastar para siempre un fanatismo nuevo

SONG FOR THE AMERICAN SOLDIERS

There they go there they go
By air by land by sea
There go the Atlases of the New World
With a hemisphere in tow
To wipe away another's tears

There they go there they go
Through the air that opens its arms to them
Across seas that swell with pride
Across sandy deserts of legend
Across the mountains

There they go there they go
Under the relentless sun that ripens their eyes
Over the snow that eases their wounds
There go the heroic lads
With their smiles open to the sky to the land and to the sea
There go the soldiers from your America Walt Whitman
There they go to great glorious sacrifice
With the world's love in their hearts

There goes the man
With the word freedom on his lips
The magic word
Greater than any mouth on earth
Deeper than any poems
Stronger than any volcano

There goes the man
On the way to his monument
To crush forever a new fanaticism

El monstruo oscuro de una atroz pesadilla
Que paladea el sufrimiento ajeno

Cantad los que tenéis la voz del canto
La voz de los grandes vientos
Cantad un himno inmenso
Que levante las almas humilladas
A su altura de antaño a su luz propia
Ahí van dulces muchachos
Que aman la vida y buscan la muerte
Para salvar al mundo
De ese temblor opaco de árboles desgraciados
Ahí van rudos muchachos

Oh jóvenes dioses
Entre palmas y flores váis entrando en la Historia
¿Es verdad que la Historia no os asusta?
Oh jóvenes atlantes
Sublimes como un cielo que se mueve más allá del cielo
Sublimes como los cinco mares cuando se dan la mano
Sublimes como la esperanza en medio del naufragio
Sublimes como la voz que saliera de un objeto y nos dijera Padre

América hermana América
Quién te llama a ti a la muerte
Sino el sentido más puro de la vida
Cómo no oír la voz de los abuelos

La voz del fundador de tan larga familia
Cuando pide socorro entre sombras furibundas
Cómo no oír la voz de la Gran Madre
Tantos meses sangrando solitaria
Bajo nubes de monstruos insaciables
Cómo no oír el llamado de las razas que gimen sobre el mapa del mundo

Ah las sombras lanzando sombras a la tierra
Ellos creían ser los más valientes
Y vosotros lo fuisteis

That dark monster out of an atrocious nightmare
That relishes the suffering of others

Sing all of you who have a singing voice
A voice from the great winds
Sing an immense hymn
To raise humiliated souls
To their former heights to their own light
There they go fine lads
Who love life yet seek death
To save the world
From that opaque trembling of doomed trees
There they go rugged lads

O young gods
Amidst palms and flowers you enter History
Is it true that History does not frighten you?
Oh young Atlases
Sublime as a sky stirring beyond the sky
Sublime as the five oceans joining hands
Sublime as hope amidst the wreckage
Sublime as the voice issuing from some object and saying Father to us

America sister America
Who summons you to death
If not the purest meaning of life
How can you not hear the voices of your ancestors

The voice of the founder of such a vast family
Calling for help amidst furious shadows
How can you not hear the voice of the Great Mother
Bleeding alone for so many months
Beneath clouds of ravenous monsters
How can one not hear the calls of sobbing races across the face of the world

Ah the shadows casting shadows on the earth
They thought themselves the bravest
But you were braver

Ellos creían ser los más tenaces y los más vigorosos
Creían tener más juventud más entusiasmo
Pero vosotros depasasteis su medida
Sin gritos sin alardes sin teatrales posturas
Vosotros vais a rescatar al hombre
Como aquellos cruzados de otros siglos
Que buscaban el sepulcro de un dios

Hombre qué haces con tus puertas cerradas
No oyes el estruendo de cien mil olas irritadas
No oyes un yunque fabuloso de truenos y relámpagos
Es América en marcha al sacrificio de la gloria
Es América que va a castigar las tiranías
Es América que está rompiendo a martillazos
Las cadenas que ataban ciudades y montañas
Es una legión de héroes escalando la Historia
Son los leones de la palabra Libertad
Que llevan en sus manos el destino
Como un niño lloroso
Que se había perdido en las tinieblas

Libertad he ahí tu nombre Libertad
Floreciendo al paso de los nuevos atlantes
Libertad otra vez en el aire y en la tierra
Madurando en la punta de los árboles
Libertad respirada por las bocas sedientas
Libertad en la luz de los ojos que aplauden
Cabalgata sublime de una sola palabra
Que encierra toda el alma del hombre
La sangre interminable de tantas epopeyas

Que no venga la muerte antes de ver tu triunfo
Antes de oír la voz del hombre libre
Sin angustias de sombra enfurecida
Mas si mi vida oh Libertad te es necesaria
A tus plantas está sólo a tus plantas
Aunque no vea el alba que agita sus banderas
Como una selva enamorada de la gloria

They thought themselves the most tenacious the most vigorous
They thought they had more youth more enthusiasm
But you exceeded their measure
No shouting, no boasting, no theatrical poses
You go to rescue humanity
Like those crusaders from centuries past
Who sought the tomb of a god

Man what are you doing with your doors closed
Do you not hear the roar of a hundred thousand raging waves
Do you not hear a fabulous anvil of thunder and lightning
It is America marching to the sacrifice of glory
It is America setting out to punish tyranny
It is America hammering apart
The chains that bound cities and mountains
It is a legion of heroes scaling the heights of History
They are the lions of the word Freedom
Carrying destiny in their hands
Like a weeping child
That had been lost in the darkness

Liberty behold thy name Liberty
Flourishing in the wake of the new Atlases
Liberty once again in the air and on the earth
Ripening at the tops of trees
Liberty inhaled through thirsty mouths
Liberty in the light of applauding eyes
Sublime cavalcade of a single word
Encapsulating the entire soul of mankind
The endless blood of so many epics

May death not come before it sees you triumph
Before it hears the voice of free men
With no fear of the furious shadows
But, if, O Liberty, you have need of my life
It lies at your feet only at your feet
Even if I do not see the dawn waving its banners
Like a forest in love with glory

ALEGORÍA DE BOLÍVAR

I

Muchacho ¡cómo te latía el corazón! Sentado bajo un árbol venezolano en la noche contemplabas las estrellas que significan algo y sentías el llamado de tu tierra natal.

Y sentías el rumor de los llanos más allá de tu jardín y el ruido de las grandes montañas como un resplandor y el ruido lejano de las selvas que conjuran la noche y el rumor de los ríos que parecen llevar un tambor ronco al fondo de las aguas.

¿Por qué latía tanto tu corazón?

El soñador tenía un árbol para hacer techo a sus sueños, y para murmurar la misma frase de tierra, las mismas palabras o tal vez peticiones de suelo nativo que quiere romper cadenas y saludar al sol.

Oh tristeza de las hojas al nivel del cielo. Oh esperanza de las raíces en su larga noche.

Era esbelto como la palabra Héroe y tenía ojos de relámpago libertador. Se llamaba Simón.

La cabeza erguida parecía estar contando planetas. En la garganta sentía el gusto amargo de la tempestad que se avecina.

El ensueño entornaba los párpados y alguna repentina imagen violenta volvía a levantarlos y dilataba las pupilas.

Aspiraba la noche en voluptuosos tragos de oscuridad brillante.

Su tierra se extendía como dos alas a derecha e izquierda de su corazón. Y más allá de su tierra las otras tierras hermanas. Y todas le llamaban por su nombre en las noches tan lentas. Y todas le hablaban en las sombras.

Su corazón se dilataba. Sus ojos adquirían un fulgor tremendo.

Su corazón se dilataba de un modo pavoroso. Su corazón tomaba la forma de un continente.

ALLEGORY OF BOLÍVAR

I

Young man, how your heart throbbed! Seated under a Venezuelan tree one night you gazed at stars that meant something and you felt the call of your native land.

And you could hear the murmur of the plains beyond your garden and the sounds of great mountains like a glimmer and the distant sound of forests conjuring up the night and the murmur of rivers that seemed to carry a hoarse drum deep within their waters.

Why did his heart beat so hard?

The dreamer had a tree to shelter his dreams, and to murmur the same earthy phrases, the same words or perhaps pleas from the native soil yearning to break its chains and greet the sun.

O the sadness of sky-high leaves! O the hope of roots during their long night!

He was slender as the word Hero with eyes like the lightning of liberation. His name was Simón.

His upright head seemed to be counting planets. In his throat he felt the bitter taste of the coming storm.

Dreams would narrow his eyelids and yet some sudden violent image would open them again and would widen his pupils.

He breathed in the night with lusty gulps of brilliant darkness.

His land stretched out like two wings to right and left of his heart. And beyond his land there were sister lands. And all called out his name during those slow nights. And they all spoke to him in the shadows.

His heart swelled. His eyes burned with an immense glow.

His heart swelled frighteningly. His heart took on the form of a continent.

II

Simón Bolívar. Tu nombre ha atravesado toda América en un áspero galope.

Los tejados de mil pueblos ven pasar su caballo como una noche por la noche. Y ven allá lejos tu mano descorrer el alba.

Aliento de millones de gargantas de grandes pueblos apretados como racimos cósmicos que te saludan y te aplauden.

Oh alegría de liberar del libertador.

Alegría de crear del creador.

Alegría de soñar del soñador.

Era preciso que el esclavo levantara la frente.

Y contemplara el mundo como un enfermo que sale a la orilla del mar.

III

América dormida, envuelta en olas que hacen crujir sus huesos y enormes remolinos

América levanta la cabeza. La bella nadadora entre dos océanos suntuosos.

Levanta la cabeza.

Un huracán vertiginoso sacude sus espaldas tan adornadas como el cielo.

América resuena de marchas militares y de cantos fúnebres.

Los ríos son arterias de sangre valerosa y pulsos de agonía. Los árboles son llamas de entusiasmo.

Se cruzan los ejércitos atentos a la noche y entregados al día. Polvaredas de marchas y contramarchas. Orgías de la muerte y delirio de victorias.

Bolívar a caballo saludado por dos mil volcanes.

Bolívar a caballo en la aurora que asoma en todas las montañas.

Orgullo de las selvas cantando un himno más grande que el sol en su trozo de cielo.

Resplandor de las hogueras velando en los desfiladeros y en los llanos impacientes de momentos de gloria.

Al anuncio del Centauro se preparan las flores. Al paso del jinete infatigable nacen rosas y campanadas.

II

Simón Bolívar. Your name has galloped roughshod across the whole of America.

The roofs of a thousand villages see your horse go by like a night in the night-time. And they see your hand far away drawing back the dawn.

The breath from millions of throats from great peoples pressed together like cosmic clusters saluting you and applauding you.

Oh the liberator's joy in liberation!

The creator's joy in creation.

The dreamer's joy in dreaming.

It was necessary for the slave lift his head.

To gaze upon the world like a sick man leaving for the shores of the sea.

III

America asleep, wrapped in bone-crunching waves and huge whirlpools.

America raises its head. A beautiful swimmer between two sumptuous oceans.

It raises its head.

A whirling hurricane shakes its shoulders adorned as richly as the heavens.

America resounds with military marches and funeral dirges.

Its rivers are arteries of brave blood and pulses of agony. Its trees are flames of enthusiasm.

Armies march and counter-march, attentive to the night and devoted to the day. Clouds of dust from marching back and forth. Orgies of death and delirious victories.

Bolívar on horseback saluted by two thousand volcanoes.

Bolívar on horseback in the dawn that peeps over all the mountains.

The pride of the forests sings a hymn greater than the sun in its patch of sky.

Glowing bonfires watch over mountain passes and impatient plains awaiting moments of glory.

When the Centaur is announced, flowers are prepared. In the wake of the tireless rider roses bloom and bells ring.

El huracán Bolívar no reposa. Vencido o vencedor no se fatiga ni conoce el desaliento.

Banderas visionarias tremolan sobre la audacia electrizada de los vientos.

El huracán exclama: «Si la naturaleza se opone, lucharemos contra ella y haremos que obedezca.»

Con tan mínimos recursos este jinete en su caballo audaz realiza empresa tan enorme.

América romperá sus primeras cadenas y quedará aguardando otro Centauro para romperlas todas.

Oh, glorioso. Pero he aquí tu gran gloria:

Por primera vez en todo el continente, antes que el arco-iris se levante con sus ropas de lujo, declaras la Abolición de la Esclavitud. Y la tierra fue azul y se encendieron lámparas como flores en los ojos.

Oh admirado, he aquí otra admiración: tu frente de mármol en medio del infortunio.

Y tu tenacidad.

Tu tenacidad inagotable.

Tu tenacidad de océano llamando al infinito.

Es en el desastre en donde siento el incendio de tus venas.

Y el vagido anunciador de la borrasca. La nueva racha, la próxima siembra del pavor en praderas de triunfo resonante de alaridos y cascos de potros desbocados.

Ni un minuto desfallece. El torrente no está quieto jamás hasta alcanzar su gran designio.

Simón allí estaba América gimiendo como una enorme flor entre sus mares encadenados

Y tú te ofreciste a los pueblos como un leño macizo.

IV

Ahora te preguntan tus estatuas: «¿Cumpliste con la ley de tu día histórico?».

Y tú crees que sí. Y tal vez la razón sea contigo.

Simón, hay tinieblas sobre el mundo. Aún reina la noche en tus Américas.

There is no rest for hurricane Bolívar. Victorious or vanquished, he does not tire nor does he get discouraged.

Visionary banners flutter in the electrified daring of the winds.

The hurricane proclaims: "If nature opposes us, we will fight her and make her obey."

With minimal resources this rider on his bold horse undertakes an immense task.

America will break its first chains and await another Centaur to break the rest.

Oh, glorious one! But here is your great glory:

For the first time on the entire continent, before the rainbow rises in its fancy clothes, you declared the Abolition of Slavery. And the earth turned blue and lanterns lit up like flowers in our eyes.

Oh, admirable man! Here is another thing to admire: your marble brow when in the midst of misfortune.

And your tenacity.

Your inexhaustible tenacity.

Your oceanic tenacity calling out to infinity.

It is in disaster that I feel the fire in your veins.

And the cry heralding the storm. The latest gust of wind, the next one sowing seeds of terror in fields of triumph echoing with screams and the hooves of runaway colts.

Not for a moment does he falter. The torrent is never calm until its great purpose is fulfilled.

Simón, America was there, moaning like a huge flower between its chained seas.

And you offered yourself to its people like a massive vessel.

IV

Now your statues ask you: "Did you comply with the laws of your historic day?"

And you think you have. And perhaps you have the right of it.

Simón, there is darkness falling over the world. Night still reigns in your Americas.

Hoy los hombres estamos empeñados en libertar al hombre de una esclavitud igual si no mayor a la que tú rompiste. Estamos batallando por una libertad más alta que la tuya.

La libertad a que aspiramos busca en estas tierras un nuevo y gran Libertador.

Pronto, Simón, desata tus amarras de las sombras, desenvaina tu espada color lluvia bienhechora y toma tu sitio en nuestras filas.

Ahí está tu caballo de ijares impacientes, vibrando como un gran violín de marsellesas y cantos resucitados. Ahí está esperando tu caballo

Y detrás millones de jinetes como olas efervescentes.

Pronto nuestras montañas saludarán el alba que se acerca con un rumor de pasos milenarios que vienen desde el fondo de la historia como una interminable procesión de esqueletos heroicos.

Today we men are bent on freeing humanity from a bondage as great, if not greater, than the one you broke. We are battling for liberty higher than yours.

The liberty to which we aspire calls for a great new Liberator in these lands.

Soon, Simón, break loose from the shadows, unsheathe your generous rain-coloured sword and take your place in our ranks.

Your horse is there with impatient flanks, quivering like a great violin with *Marseillaises* and resurrected songs. There your horse awaits you.

And behind it millions of riders like foaming waves.

Soon our mountains will greet the approaching dawn with a rumble of ancient footsteps rising from the depths of history like an endless procession of heroic skeletons.

MARCA REGISTRADA

Las células amenazan el pensamiento
Amenazan el jardín endiosado
La mano donde empieza el mundo
Donde se escriben los acontecimientos
A través de la sangre de los sexos y los bosques

Las olas se levantan retratando a los hijos
Y mueren en su esencia
Sin vacilar de frase
En la fecha exacta
Van y vienen por su misma esencia
Con sus nervios orgullosos
A flor de pensamiento
A flor de flor
A flor de sentimiento
A flor de tristeza

Todo es tiempo final
Como la selva que cree en los embrujos
Y se atormenta de rayos
Y grandes gotas hirvientes que caen como el cielo

Todo es tiempo sin fin
Como los arroyos en el sueño
Y el calor demasiado rápido
De las lágrimas huyendo
A través de las edades

Las células amenazan el pensamiento
Donde correspondía un paisaje afiebrado
Donde ya no hay frontera
Ni mano que escriba la última palabra

REGISTERED TRADEMARK

Cells threaten thought
Threaten the deified garden
The hand where the world begins
Where events are written down
Through the blood of sexes and forests

Waves rise up portraying their children
And die in their essence
With no hesitation of speech
On the exact date
They come and go by their very essence
With their proud nerves
At the level of thought
At the level of a flower
At the level of feeling
At the level of sorrow

Here we are in the end times
Like the forest that believes in spells
And is tormented by lightning
And great scalding drops that fall like the sky

Here we are in time without end
Like streams in a dream
And the overly swift heat
Of tears fleeing
Through the ages

Cells threaten thought
Where a fevered landscape once belonged
Where there are no longer borders
Nor a hand to write the final word

POÈMES INÉDITS EN FRANÇAIS

POEMAS INÉDITOS EN FRANCÉS

UNCOLLECTED POEMS IN FRENCH

POÈME

Fille
Dans la vie
On attend

Il y a un chemin
Où meurent les soirs
Quelqu'un vient

POEM

Girl
In life
One waits

There is a path
Where evenings die
Someone is coming

POÈME

Quelqu'un vient de mourir en moi
Et une cloche imperceptible
Me parle à l'oreille

Une étoile oubliée
Pleure dans l'obscurité
Sur le lac plus profond que la terre
Où toutes les barques ont coulé

Là-bas sous l'ombre
Le fauteuil qui attendait le retour
A été occupé

POEM

Someone is coming to die inside me
And an unobtrusive bell
Whispers in my ear

A forgotten star
Weeps in the darkness
On the lake deeper than the earth
Where all the boats have sunk

Down there beneath the shadow
The armchair that awaits my return
Has been taken

FENÊTRE

Sur la cheminée la gondole porte des fleurs naufrages
Le portrait de Marie est fait par l'Homme noir
Le soleil caressera les lèvres
Mais c'est pour moi la bouche de la mort
Parle tout bas!
Les flammes qui brûlent ton âme
S'arrêtent parfois l'oreille parle tout bas
Les cierges du piano veillent encore la voix
Le livre du tapis brûlé par l'homme noir
Montant au mirador surveille son départ
Les mots qu'il avait dit tombait à notre route
Vélo de Véronique et que le vent secoue
L'ombre des boucles d'oreille sur le cou!
Les brèches endossaient la cendre lourde
Et la bonne en cachette allait au cinéma
L'Hiver et l'Homme Noir! Contre eux le chien aboie
Le portrait de Marie!
Marie et celui du grand-père égoïste.

Vincent Huidobro
Max Jacob

WINDOW

On the mantelpiece the gondola bears shipwrecked flowers
The portrait of Marie is painted by the Black Man
The sun will caress her lips
But for me that is the mouth of death
Speak softly!
The flames that burn your soul
Sometimes catch your ear speak softly
The candles on the piano still watch over your voice
The carpet book burned by the black man
Climbing the watchtower observes his departure
The words he had uttered fell onto our road
Berenice's bicycle shaken by the wind
The shadow of earrings hanging on your neck!
The breaches were covered in heavy ash
And the chambermaid used to sneak into the cinema
Winter and the Black Man! The dog barks at them
The portrait of Marie!
Marie and the one of her selfish grandfather.

Vincent Huidobro
Max Jacob

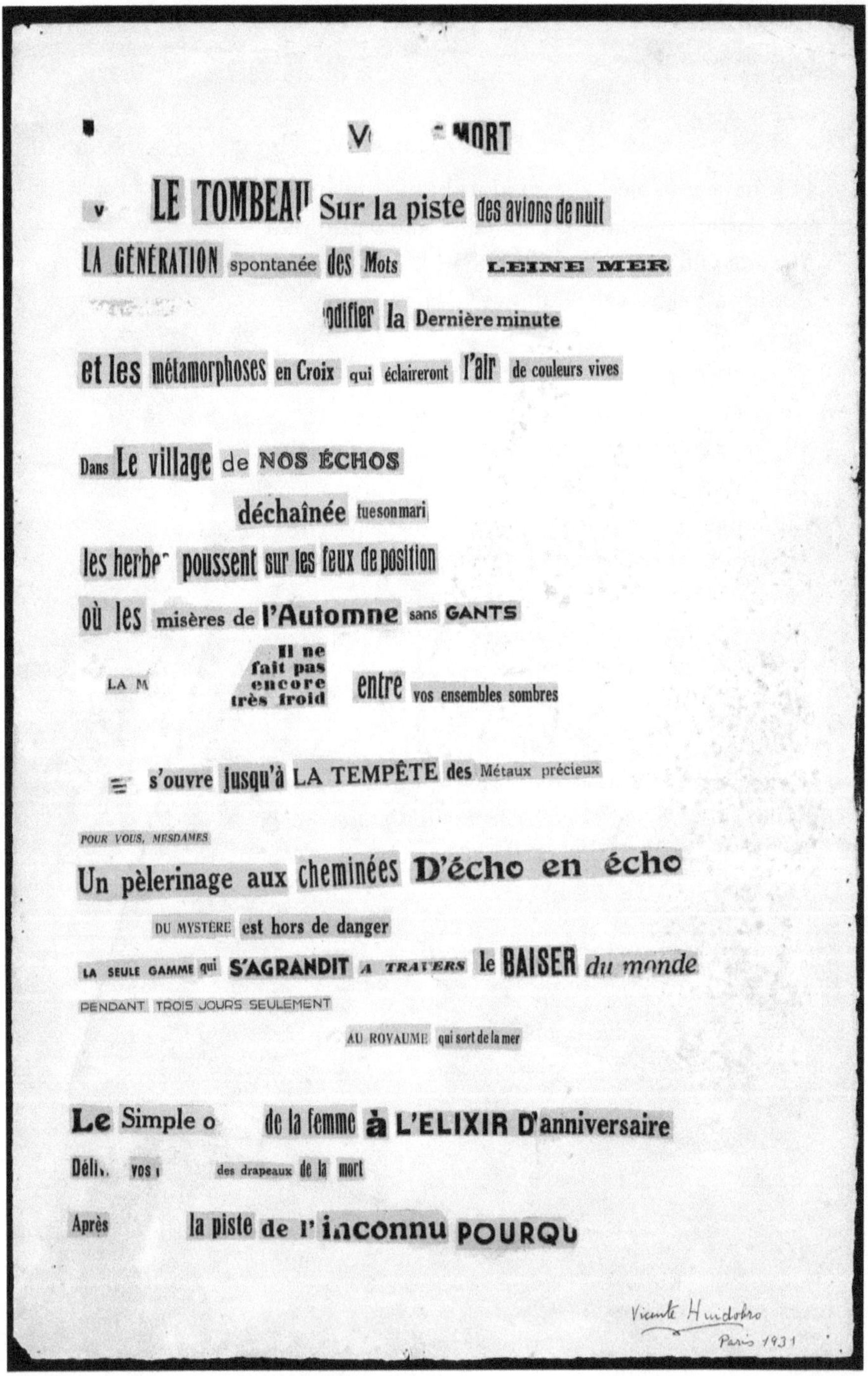

V MORT

v LE TOMBEAU Sur la piste des avions de nuit

LA GÉNÉRATION spontanée des Mots LEINE MER

odifier la Dernière minute

et les métamorphoses en Croix qui éclaireront l'air de couleurs vives

Dans Le village de NOS ÉCHOS

déchaînée tuesonmari

les herbe poussent sur les feux de position

où les misères de l'Automne sans GANTS

LA M Il ne fait pas encore très froid entre vos ensembles sombres

s'ouvre jusqu'à LA TEMPÊTE des Métaux précieux

POUR VOUS, MESDAMES

Un pèlerinage aux cheminées D'écho en écho

DU MYSTÈRE est hors de danger

LA SEULE GAMME qui S'AGRANDIT A TRAVERS le BAISER du monde

PENDANT TROIS JOURS SEULEMENT

AU ROYAUME qui sort de la mer

Le Simple o de la femme à L'ELIXIR D'anniversaire

Déli vos des drapeaux de la mort

Après la piste de l'inconnu POURQU

Vicente Huidobro
Paris 1931

DEMANDE VOTRE MORT

[v]   Le tombeau sur la piste des avions de nuit
La génération spontanée des mots   [?ha]leine mer
                                        [m]odifier la dernière minute
et les métamorphoses en croix qui éclaireront l'air de couleurs vives

Dans le village de nos échos
                        déchaînée tue son mari
les herbes poussent sur les feux de position
où les misères de l'Automne sans gants
                            Il ne
                            fait pas
La m[   ]   encore
                        très froid   entre vos ensembles sombres

[   ] s'ouvre jusqu'à la tempête des métaux précieux

pour vous, mesdames

Un pèlerinage aux cheminées d'écho en écho
        du mystère est hors de danger
La seule gamme qui s'agrandit à travers le baiser du monde
pendant trois jours seulement
                                        au royaume qui sort de la mer

Le simple o[   ] de la femme à l'élixir d'anniversaire
Déli[vrer?] vos [   ] des drapeaux de la mort
Après [   ] la piste de l'inconnu pourqu[oi]

ASK FOR YOUR DEATH

[ ] The tomb on the runway of the night aeroplanes
The spontaneous generation of words ?breath sea
?modify the last minute
and the metamorphosis into crosses that will brighten the air with colour

In the village of our echoes
woman unleashed kills her husband
the grass grows over the navigation lights
where the miseries of Autumn without gloves
It is
not yet
The [??] very
cold amongst your dark outfits

[ ] opens up to the storm of precious metals

for you, ladies

A pilgrimage to the chimneys from echo to echo
of the mystery is out of danger
The only range that expands through the kiss of the world
for three days only
to the kingdom rising from the sea

The simple [ ] of the woman with the birthday elixir
Deliver[?] your [ ] from the flags of death
After [ ] the trail of the unknown why

NOTES

Details of Original Publication of the Poems

Key

Índice = *Índice de la nueva poesía americana*, ed. Alberto Hidalgo, Jorge Luis Borges & Vicente Huidobro (Buenos Aires & Mexico City: Sociedad de Publicaciones El Inca, 1926).
Antología 1935 = *Antología de la nueva poesía chilena*, ed. Eduardo Anguita & Volodia Teitelboim (Santiago: Editorial Zig-Zag. 1935).
Antología 1945 = *Antología de Vicente Huidobro* (Santiago: Editorial Zig-Zag, 1945), ed. Eduardo Anguita.
Montes 1989 = Hugo Montes, 'Poemas inéditos y dispersos de Vicente Huidobro', *Revista Chilena de Literatura* N° 34, 1989.
Castro 1996 = *Poesía y poética, 1911–1948*, ed. René de Castro, (Madrid: Alianza Editorial, 1996).
OPF = *Obras poéticas en francés*, ed. Waldo Rojas (Santiago: Editorial Universitaria, 1999).
OP = *Obra poética*, ed. Cedomil Goic (Paris: Éditions ALLCA XX, 2003).

Early Poems

'Triángulo armónico' and 'La capilla aldeana' were published in the author's *Canciones en la noche* (Santiago: Imprenta y Encuadernación Chile, 1913). The first of these had appeared previously in Huidobro's own magazine, *Musa Joven,* 6 (Santiago, October 1912).

'Vaguedad subconsciente' appeared in *Ideales* (Concepción, July 1915). The other poems in the *Uncollected Poems 1913–1916* section were printed in OP, one of which ("Una poesía que haga sentir…") was first identified and given an approximate dating by Hugo Montes (see Montes 1989), the second editor of Huidobro's collected works. 'Ocaso en el espejo' was first printed in Castro 1996.

Song for Lindbergh

This poem, previously referred to in all commentaries under its Spanish title, 'Canto a Lindbergh', dates from 1927, and was written by Huidobro while he was staying in New York, and visiting movie companies (as well as winning a prize for his film treatment of *Cagliostro*). The poem's only previous appearance in a book was in the form of three illegible thumbnail photos in the special triple issue of *Poesía* (ed. René de Costa, Madrid, 1991) devoted to Huidobro. The photos were accompanied by the editor's translation of the text *back* into Spanish.

Although it has usually been claimed that the poem had not been published in *any* form prior to its appearance in *Poesía*, Pedro Marqués de Armas – in his blog *Hotel Telégrafo*[1] – records the previously unrecognised fact that a Spanish version did in fact appear in fairly short order (the flight having occurred on 30 May 1927) in a major Havana newspaper, the *Diario de la Marina*, on 31 July 1927. The newspaper's byline stated that the poem had been obtained for them by Dr. Gonzalo Aróstegui (1859–1940), a prominent Cuban expatriate then based in New York. Huidobro had been interviewed in the same newspaper the year before, while passing through Havana, and thus may have been well-disposed towards the *Diario*. Marqués printed a transcription on his blog,[2] and provided a scanned version of the original newspaper text in a downloadable PDF "dossier".[3] The Havana publication managed to escape the notice of the editors of OP2003, and indeed every other compiler of Huidobro's poetry.

One final oddity is that the poet is referred to in the *Diario* with his legal patronymic, García Huidobro (*sic*, without the hyphen), rather than by his simplified pen-name, Huidobro. He had been using the latter since 1914. On formal occasions he would have been introduced as Sr. García-Huidobro, which might explain the name's appearance in this fashion, if Aróstegui had indeed received it from the author in New York. Aróstegui was over thirty years older than our poet, something of a grandee, and a highly respected medical man, and it would thus have been normal for there to have been a degree of formality to their encounter. I could also be over-thinking this: the first typescript of the English translation included in this book shows two corrections to the author's name – firstly, the N of his French name, Vincent, has been scored out, and, secondly, I assume that the scoring-out before "Huidobro" removes the word "García". If the Spanish typescript given to Aróstegui was identical in its presentation, then the author's full name may well have been present.

[1] https://hoteltelegrafo.blogspot.com/2024/06/el-poema-que-huidobro-publico-en-la.html, 16 June, 2024. Accessed 18 December 2024.

[2] https://hoteltelegrafo.blogspot.com/2024/06/canto-lindbergh-original-de-huidobro.html Accessed 18 December 2024.

[3] https://drive.google.com/file/d/1aFbCQi_eNkEU8LEUGMgbG12F5B-1w2A0w/view

Taking the handwritten comment at the top-right corner of the first page of the English typescript ("translated from the Spanish") at face value, we must take it that Huidobro wrote the poem in Spanish first, and then created the English version later. The rationale for this may well originate in his announcement to the press that some of his substantial prize money for the *Cagliostro* film treatment was to be donated to a monument in honour of Lindbergh. If the translation were intended for this, it would explain some of the changes – above all, the reference in the Spanish version to France's supremacy in aviation, albeit now challenged by Lindbergh's achievement.

The second typescript included here is a version of which I was unaware until the Fundación Huidobro and the Universidad Católica de Chile kindly provided a copy. It appears to be a later version, as it is a clean copy of what appears to be a finished text, and differs from the first one in several places.

There is no record of any other text in English by Huidobro, but I think we can assume he could read English well enough, as well as get by in English conversation. One wonders if any of his friends in New York might have helped with the translation of the poem, just as Gris, Picabia and Reverdy had helped him with his French back in 1917. Obvious errors aside, some clumsy phrasing, and infelicitous word choices, remain here and there, which suggests a native speaker was not responsible for the entire text – although it is also plausible that a native speaker *with no ear for poetry* helped generate the English version.

Occasional Poems

Poems in this section that saw publication before OP2003 are follows: 'Pasión pasión y muerte' first appeared as 'Pasión y muerte' in *La Nación*, Santiago, 2 April 1926. It was reprinted under its revised title in *Antología* 1945. 'Elegía a la muerte de Lenin' first appeared in *Antología* 1935, bearing the date 1924 in its title, that being the year of Lenin's death; 'Canto al Primero de Mayo in *Mástil*, 4 (Santiago, 7 August 1933), under the title 'Un poema revolucionario' (A Revolutionary Poem); 'URSS' in *Principios* (Santiago, November 1935); 'La dulzura de vivir' in *Onda corta*, 5:5 (Santiago, 22 January 1936); 'Policías y soldados' in *La Opinión* (Santiago, 1935); 'Está sangrando España' in *Escritores y Artistas Chilenas a la España Popular* (Santiago: Imprenta y Encuadernación Marion, 1936); 'Gloria y sangre' in *Madre España. Homenaje de los poetas chilenos* (Santiago: Editorial

Panorama, 1937); 'España' in *El Mono Azul*, 20, (Madrid, 1937); 'Pasionaria' in *Hora de España*, VII (Valencia, July 1937)'; 'Fuera de aquí' in *La Opinión* (Santiago, 14 October 1937); 'Tchu-De' in *Frente Popular* (Santiago, 3 November 1937; 'Canto a Francia' in *La Hora* (Santiago, 2 June 1940), and then reprinted in the anthology *Francia* (Santiago: Zig Zag, 1943); 'Canto a los soldados americanos' in Braulio Arenas's edition of Huidobro's collected works in 1964.

It should be noted that several of these occasional poems were unearthed by Hugo Montes (see Montes 1989) before their inclusion in OP. This essay and mini-anthology of allegedly uncollected Huidobro poems is however marred by a number of errors: for instance, Montes included some poems that had in fact already appeared in *Últimos poemas* (1948) and *Ver y palpar* (1941), and also presents several lines from a poem that had originally appeared in *Poemas árticos* (1918) – and was later republished in *Índice* (1926) in this same truncated form – as "uncollected". The error in the republished poem in *Índice*, if indeed it is one, rather than simply a revision – where the original title and the first two lines have disappeared – can almost certainly be explained by the fact that the new title, printed all in caps, was *already* all in caps in the original, *but as the poem's third line*. Irregular capitalisation and spatially-arranged text were features of the poet's work in 1917–18, under the influence of Apollinaire, and it is quite possible that the layout was misunderstood by the anthology's typesetters, if they were unused to setting modern poetry.

'Alegoría de Bolívar' was printed in *Cuadernos del Sur*, 3 (Buenos Aires, 1964) as a long-lined poem, and as prose in both the Arenas (1964) and Montes (1976) editions of Huidobro's collected works. Given that the author's typescript of this poem may now be consulted online at the Biblioteca Nacional de Chile, which categorically shows it as prose, I have decided to follow the typescript, but nonetheless still include it here amongst the poems, given that its style is of a piece with the other praise poems. I should add that the typescript displays erratic punctuation, which I have left unchanged in the Spanish text, but I have punctuated the translation differently. The text in OP – which, oddly, also presents the text as a long-lined poem – leaves out two lines, which I assume to be an error, as no explanation is given for their absence. As the manuscript shows a partial textual repetition in each of those lines, the editor of OP may have been misled. I have also corrected a couple of typos: *talvez* has been amended to *tal vez*; *hijares* has been amended to *ijares*, and I have removed some misplaced accents.

'Marca registrada' was not published in the author's lifetime, and appeared as a manuscript facsimile in *Atentado celeste: Facsimilares* (Santiago: LOM Ediciones & DIBAM, 2001). It was later reprinted in the OP2003. The manuscript is in the Biblioteca Nacional de Chile, Santiago. It is unclear when the poem was written, but the Library lists it as having been written "in Paris between 1930 and 1939", notwithstanding the fact that for most of those years Huidobro was in Santiago, rather than in Paris: he left Paris in late 1932, and returned for only a short time during the Spanish Civil War, in the Spring of 1937. His next visit would be in 1944. It is thus more than likely that it dates date from the period 1930–32.

Textual Notes

Song for Lindbergh

I have translated *bandada* (most often "flock" – as in sheep) here as "echelon", as there is a specifically Chilean usage of *bandada* to mean aircraft flying in formation. "Echelon" refers to a formation in which one plane leads with all others staggered back from it on one side.

Pasión pasión y muerte

On its first publication, this poem was titled simply 'Pasión y muerte'.

Pasionaria

La Pasionaria was the name by which Dolores Ibárruri (Isidora Dolores Ibárruri Gómez, 1895–1989) was known during the Spanish Civil War. The epithet means "the passionate one", owing to the rousing nature of her speeches, and her inspired slogan "No pasarán" (They shall not pass), coined during the battle for Madrid. She was General Secretary of the Communist Party of Spain from 1942–1960, and member of the Cortes Generales (Parliament) for Asturias, 1936–39 and again 1977–79.

Zhu De

Zhu De (1886–1976) was the founder of the Chinese Red Army, and was one of China's most significant military leaders of the 20th century. He led the defeated forces of the Nanchang Uprising (1927) south to Fujian, and then on to Hunan province, where he linked up with Mao Zedong. He was commander in chief of the Chinese Red Army throughout the Long March

(1934–35), and was later in overall command of all communist military operations against, first, the Kuomintang, and then the Japanese occupying forces. When the civil war resumed after the defeat of the Japanese, he led the renamed People's Liberation Army against the nationalist Kuomintang and drove them from the mainland. He remained in charge of the PLA until 1954.

Alegoría de Bolívar

Simón Bolívar (1783–1830) – full name, Simón José Antonio de la Santísima Trinidad Bolívar Palacios Ponte y Blanco – was born in Caracas, Venezuela, and became a military officer and statesman. He led what are now the nations of Colombia, Venezuela, Ecuador, Peru, Panama and Bolivia to independence from the Spanish Empire.

Fenêtre

This poem dates from 1925, according to OP, and was written by Huidobro with Max Jacob, apparently as an *exquisite corpse*, i.e. each man wrote one line alternately – and immediately, using the first thing that came into his head. I assume the first line is Huidobro's, given the presence of the word "naufrages", an oft-repeated image of his. Photo-reproductions of the manuscript, without transcriptions, were published in OPF and OP, but OPF did offer a Spanish translation, which has proved most helpful in deciphering two or three almost illegible words. Given Huidobro's public attack on Surrealism's "craze for automatic writing" as a kind of family parlour game, it seems a little odd that he would have engaged here in precisely such a game. The biographical record, such as it is, offers us little information on the poet's relationship with Jacob, although they had known one another since Huidobro's arrival in Paris in late 1916 and they had both been involved with the magazine *Nord-Sud*, edited by Reverdy, as well as with the Cubist painters – at one time, Jacob had been Picasso's flatmate in Paris, and was one of the painter's earliest and most devoted supporters.

Demande votre mort

As the collage indicates, this poem dates from 1931 and was evidently assembled by Huidobro while he was in Paris, using cuttings from local newspapers. I have not seen any commentary on the poem.

www.ingramcontent.com/pod-product-compliance
Lightning Source LLC
Chambersburg PA
CBHW032023050726
47590CB00006B/2276
9781848618183